THE PROMISE AND THE PRODUCT

THE PROMISE AND THE PRODUCT

200 YEARS OF AMERICAN ADVERTISING POSTERS

VICTOR MARGOLIN, IRA BRICHTA
VIVIAN BRICHTA

MACMILLAN PUBLISHING CO., INC.

NEW YORK

COLLIER MACMILLAN PUBLISHERS

LONDON

Macmillan Publishing Co., Inc.
866 Third Avenue, New York, N.Y. 10022
Collier Macmillan Canada, Ltd.

Library of Congress Cataloging in Publication Data
Margolin, Victor, 1941-
The promise and the product.
1. Posters.   2. Advertising, Outdoor—United
States—History.   3. Advertising—United States—
History.   4. Commercial products—United States—
History.   I. Brichta, Ira, joint author.   II. Brichta,
Vivian, joint author.   III. Title.
HF5843.M37   659.13'42   79-18024
ISBN 0-02-579480-9

First Printing 1979

Designed by James Udell

Printed in the United States of America

The Burma Shave verses reprinted on pages 82 and 83 are taken from Frank Rowsome, Jr.,
The Verse by the Side of the Road: The Story of the Burma Shave Signs and Jingles.
(Brattleboro, VT: Stephen Greene Press, 1965).

CONTENTS

VI

ACKNOWLEDGMENTS

VII

INTRODUCTION

1

CHAPTER ONE

Independence, Inventions, and the
Tobacco Economy: 1776–1865

21

CHAPTER TWO

Wild Claims and Brand Names:
1865–1900

61

CHAPTER THREE

Bullets, Beggars, and Bathtub Gin:
1900–1945

117

CHAPTER FOUR

Little Cars and Big Macs:
1945–1976

147

BIBLIOGRAPHY

149

INDEX

ACKNOWLEDGMENTS

Since posters mirror the era and place that gave them birth, America's advertisements offer a rich visual record of the phenomenal growth of our energetic industrial society. Their bright and vital imagery helps us experience the culture of our country on a new level. Their often naive slogans and overt claims never cease to fascinate, and their artistic motifs and regional pride remain tangible documents of our customs, styles, and attitudes. We find much artistry in the tenderly painted skin of a Victorian belle who sells beer and much sensible puritanism in the boldly pictured YMCA man of the 1920s who proclaims, "Pay your bills and be square with the world."

Today we live in an electronic age and our environment is shaped by televised advertisements. There is a distance between the thirty-second commercial and the now-historic store poster. But we can revisit yesterday and its images of our country's remarkable two-hundred-year growth by examining how advertisers have through the years communicated the promise and the product to the American public.

We would like to extend our warmest thanks to those who have helped us make this book a reality: Sylvia Margolin, a liberated muse who provided moral support and put up with a sometimes preoccupied husband, and Myra Margolin, whose generation owns the future; Congressman Sidney Yates and his executive aide Mary Bain; Julia Westerberg at The Chicago Historical Society; Robert Thall; Arthur Shay; Carl Hofmann; William and Patricia Brichta; Al Golin and Phil Richman of Golin Communications; Chris Blum of F.C.B./Honig, San Francisco; Bob Taylor of J. Walter Thompson, Chicago; David Rouse of The Chicago Public Library; Stephen Mayer of The Institute of Outdoor Advertising; Charles Sider of Foster & Kleiser, Chicago; Ruth and Lyle Mayer; Eileen LeVee; Arlene Cemeris; Patsy Rogers; and the helpful people at The Art Institute of Chicago; Metropolitan Museum of Art, New York; New York Public Library; Mercer Museum, Rhode Island Historical Society; Baker Library, Harvard University; Library of Congress; Smithsonian Institution; Needam Harper & Steers, Chicago; McCann-Erickson, Inc., Detroit; The Coca-Cola Company; Procter & Gamble. Our special thanks go to Helen Mills and to our editor, Jeanne Fredericks, for her knowledgeable guidance and patient help with the many details with which we had to deal.

Victor Margolin, Ira Brichta, Vivian Brichta
Chicago, Illinois

INTRODUCTION

The gigantic head of a young man, empty eyes staring into space, towers high above freeways and city streets across America. Each day thousands of people pass and read the adjacent message: "Winston is Taste."

The forerunner of this enormous head appeared three thousand years ago as a simple announcement of a reward for runaway slaves written on papyrus and posted on the walls of Thebes. The myriad announcements, signs, posters, and billboards descended from that papyrus have undergone many changes over the years. Roman walls were covered with a multitude of announcements. Plays and gladiatorial contests were advertised on walls in the most frequented parts of Herculaneum and Pompeii. Under the porticoes of the Pompeiian baths were notices extolling the pleasures to be found within. The gracious homes of Roman patricians usually had a portion of whitened wall, called an *album*, on which were painted or scratched notices pertinent to the affairs of the owners. Other public notices, called *libelli*, advertised the sales of estates, served notice on delinquent debtors, or announced items lost and found.

The shop or tavern sign was another kind of public announcement used by the Romans. Such signs had no words; rather they displayed a visual representation of the goods or services to be found within. A painting of Bacchus, the Roman god of wine, pressing a bunch of grapes might have hung over a Pompeiian tavern. Above their workshops, Roman tradesmen hung signs depicting the tools of their trade. A physician had a cupping glass; a surveyor, a measuring rule; and the baker's sign showed a bushel measure, a millstone, and some ears of corn.

In medieval Europe, most businesses had their distinctive signs. The preponderance of such displays in the streets of the growing cities and towns prompted one poet to write:

> Good entertainment for all that passes—
> Horses, mares, men, and asses.

The European trade signs were appealing to look at, but they also served another purpose: to communicate with a populace that was unable to read and write. The subject matter was extremely varied. Heroes and heroines, stars and planets, and all God's flora and fauna were inspiration for sign makers. Often a rebus or pun was used: a horse fording a stream for Horsford, two or three cocks for Cox, and a hare and bottle for Harebottle. Eventually, bills and posters came to advertise all sorts of events from the publication of a new book to the baiting of bears.

The principal place for bill posting in sixteenth- and seventeenth-century London was the middle aisle of Saint Paul's Cathedral, which, in addition to its function as a house of worship, was a lounging spot for idlers and newshounds and a marketplace for all manner of professionals, including pimps and procurers.

The signs grew larger and more elaborate as trade became more competitive. The narrow streets of London in that period were crowded with huge signs that obscured the sunlight. Occasionally, in stormy weather, the signs would fall, causing serious accidents to passersby. The dizzying array of signs became so confusing to London customers that a journalist wrote in the *Spectator* of 2 April 1710:

I would enjoin every shop to make use of a sign which bears some affinity to the wares in which it deals. What can be more inconsistent than to see a bawd at the sign of the Angel, or a tailor at the Lion? A cook should not live at the Boot, nor a shoemaker at the Roasted Pig; and yet, for want of this regulation, I have seen a Goat set up before the door of a perfumer, and the French King's Head at a swordcutter's.

Signs and signboards waned in the latter part of the eighteenth century. By the nineteenth, they had virtually disappeared—to be replaced by the lettered sign and the poster.

CHAPTER ONE
INDEPENDENCE, INVENTIONS, AND THE TOBACCO ECONOMY: 1776-1865

In America, signs were painted by itinerant artists who, without royalty and an aristocracy to support them, had to rely on the needs of commerce. Signboards in the New World were similar to those in England, although they were never sufficiently numerous to give American streets the colorful appearance of the crowded thoroughfares of early eighteenth-century London.

The first outdoor signs in America included the well-known tobacco shop figures of the running black boy and an Indian with a tomahawk. These are said to have originated as small counter statuettes in English tobacco shops in the early seventeenth century. The figures included Sir Walter Raleigh, a smoking Dutchman, a highlander offering his open snuff box, and others that had been used earlier in England.

Colonial innkeepers adopted the European custom of hanging a painted wooden sign from a tall pole in front of their inns. The King's Arms and The Red Lion Inn were among the favorite names. Pictorial signs in Baltimore and Philadelphia were more numerous and colorful than those in New England towns. Taverns in Southern settlements displayed many of the names common in London: The Bull and Mouth, The Seven Stars, The Golden Hare, and The Maypole. In prerevolutionary New York, clever sign painters advertised the delights of a rare sirloin steak with a quote from Shakespeare: "If it were done when 'tis done, then 'twere well it were done quickly."

In New England, the puritanical John Wesley thought that signboards should not relate "to the flesh" and ought to be "spiritualized with an intent that when a person walks along the street, instead of having his mind filled with vanity and his thoughts amused with the trifling things that continually present themselves, he may be able to think of something profitable."

Before the Revolution, the pictorial sign came into widest use in Philadelphia, then the art center of America. Artists and art students of the period made their livings painting signboards and fire buckets while they sought commissions for portraits and landscapes, which were both preferred and profitable.

Once America had gained its independence, innkeepers did away with names that reminded them of their former colonial status. Names such as the Royal Standard and The Three Crowns were replaced by the names of Revolutionary War heroes like General Wayne or George Washington. When Rip van Winkle awakened from his long sleep, he noticed that the "ruby face of King George," which once identified

New York street scene showing advertising signs, Broadway to Leonard St. Lithograph, c. 1855. Museum of the City of New York.

a familiar tavern, had been replaced by the visage of George Washington and "The red coat . . . changed for one of buff and blue. . . ."

Matthew Pratt, a pupil of the Philadelphia artist Benjamin West, was the first to gain fame for his sign painting. His most effective signboard was a painting for a Philadelphia tavern; it depicted the Federal Convention engaged in a discussion about the Constitution. Thirty-eight figures were painted on the sign. When it was mounted in front of the tavern, crowds of people were said to have gathered in the street and challenged one another to see who could identify the greatest number of delegates.

Besides tavern owners, hatters, smiths, druggists, and other tradesmen who set up shops in colonial towns also commissioned painted signs, sometimes quite elaborate ones. The sign that identified the shop of Jacob Christ, Hatter, showed a selection of elegant hats flanked by an Indian with a bow on one side and a hunting dog and fox on the other. Not content with showing hats, the artist had managed to include a tranquil landscape as well.

By the middle of the nineteenth century, the pictorial signboard had largely disappeared. A lithographed view of Broadway, published in 1855, showed a row of stores with their proprietors' names and the goods they sold written out rather than illustrated. The signs hung above the store windows or higher up on the buildings, making it possible for passersby to identify the stores from a distance.

For a long time, the pictorial signs were the principal means employed by tradesmen to advertise their wares to a populace that couldn't read. The spread of literacy in Europe and America, sparked by Johannes Gutenberg's invention of movable type in 1438, resulted in the wide use of posters, trade cards, newspapers, and other means of advertising that used text either by itself or together with pictures. William Caxton, the English printer, is credited with the first poster, a handbill knows as a *Siquis*, printed in England in 1478, only forty years after Gutenberg's invention.

Before bills and posters could be widely employed in America, an indigenous printing industry had to develop. Among the first American printers was Stephen Day, a former locksmith, who pulled his first proof in Cambridge, Massachusetts, in 1639. His first printed piece was an oath to be taken by freemen of the Bay Colony. In the early days of the colonies, printing and politics were closely allied, prompting Governor William Berkeley of Virginia to proclaim his thanks to God in 1669 that his colony still lacked printing presses.

Early bills were printed on cumbersome hand-powered presses brought from England. These soon became badly worn, but they were all the printers had until the first American type specimen books appeared in 1809.

The first successful American newspaper, the Boston *News-Letter*, had made its appearance more than a hundred years earlier, in 1704; the first advertisement followed in short order. The mutual benefit of advertising to publishers and advertisers was recognized from the beginning. The April 24, 1704 issue of the Boston *News-Letter* carried this notice:

ADVERTISEMENT

This News-Letter is to be continued weekly, and all Persons who have Houses, Lands, Tenements, Farms, Ships, Vessels, Goods, Wares or Merchandise, etc. to be Sold or Let; or Servants Run-Away, or Goods Stole or Lost; may have the same inserted at a Reasonable Rate, from Twelve Pence to Five Shillings, and not to exceed: Who may agree with John Campbel, Post-master of Boston.

It was, however, another twenty-five years before advertising began to flower through the efforts of America's first advertising genius, Benjamin Franklin, whose long list of credits includes founding the University of Pennsylvania, the public library system, and the United States Post Office;

inventing fire insurance, the stove that bears his name, bifocals, and the lightning rod. *The Pennsylvania Gazette,* which Franklin edited, soon had the largest circulation and advertising volume of any newspaper in the colonies. Franklin, who was publisher, printer, and editor of the paper, also wrote most of the advertising copy. He was the original conglomerate, writing the copy for the sale of his own inventions and publishing the notices in the paper he edited. As a copywriter, Franklin was about one hundred and fifty years ahead of his contemporaries. In the publicity for his newly invented stove, for example, he avoided a description of the product for the promise of health, comfort, and pleasure to be derived from its use. Not only did he appeal to the vanity of his customers, but he also frightened them with "specters of head colds, rheums, and shriveled skins," which resulted, he claimed, from the use of fireplaces rather than heating stoves.

By the 1830s, newspapers had begun to resemble those of today. The steam-powered press, imported from England, increased the speed of printing and lowered the cost per copy. With the efficiency brought about by printing from cylinders, larger circulations became practical. Before 1833, no paper had reached a circulation of five thousand, but with the greater printing efficiency, circulation could be increased while the per-copy price could be reduced below the accepted six cents. The new one-cent dailies attracted a wide readership in the large towns. Part of their popularity resulted from the invention of the telegraph by Samuel Morse, which made improved newspaper coverage of distant events and eyewitness accounts possible by the 1840s.

The growing dependence of the large-circulation newspapers on advertisers had its problems. The New York *Herald* developed a reputation for accepting thinly veiled or even quite candid advertisements of prostitutes and houses of assignation. Many country papers were dependent for their existence on advertisements for elixir of snakeroot, wizard oil, and other quack remedies.

Until the epoch of the penny papers, editors generally did not print ads that broke the black column rule that ran down the center of the page. Advertisements two columns wide or news stories set in double-column were virtually nonexistent. In 1836, the New York *Herald* set ads in multicolumn widths for its major advertisers. This so enraged the smaller advertisers that the *Herald* banned all display ads for a number of years.

As the papers took a bolder approach to advertising display and news coverage, the large wooden display types created for posters began to be used for newspaper advertisements and headlines. The larger type was used for the sensational headlines that reached their peak in the "yellow press" of the late nineteenth century.

The woodcut was the earliest form of printed picture in America. John Foster, a colonial printmaker, is credited with making the first one in the United States: a portrait of the Reverend Richard Mather, which he cut in 1670. By 1700, engraving on copper plates had replaced wood engraving as a fine art form and the woodcut became widely used for commercial purposes, particularly for stock printer's cuts and newspaper logotypes. The printer's cut, first used for newspaper advertisements, soon appeared on posters as well.

The first posters in America were announcements of sales, auctions, and other such events. They had no illustrations. A bill printed by F. Bailey for John Creigh in 1785 announced that the Philadelphia merchant had received in his store a new shipment of goods from abroad. These included various kinds of broadcloth, silks, shoe buckles, metal buttons, brass and iron wire, and a selection of

John Creigh, retail merchant, Philadelphia. Broadside, 12½" × 7¾", c. 1785. Chicago Historical Society.

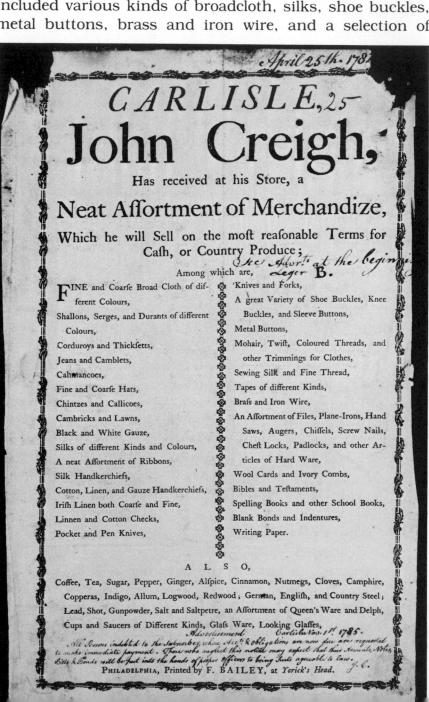

"Bibles and Testaments"; also assorted spices, coffee, tea, and "cups and saucers of different kinds." Another poster from 1803 announced a sale of valuable goods from Russia and the auction of a sailing ship that was "well founded in every Respect and could be put to Sea at very small Expense."

Posters in the colonial period advertised the business of the few enterprising settlers who had become wealthy from fur trapping, whaling, and trade with the West Indies. Most Americans, however, were not in trade but were farmers, craftsmen, and small tradesmen. Outside the cities, few merchants could supply the foods and household goods that were needed, and, as a result, the settlers learned to provide for their own needs. Many had been farmers in England and knew how to cultivate the fertile land they found in America. With the primitive implements and seeds they brought with them, they planted and harvested a rich array of grains, fruits, and vegetables, and raised livestock.

In America the settlers found many kinds of plants that

Public auction sign from Providence, Rhode Island. Broadside, c. 1803. Rhode Island Historical Society.

Sales of valuable RUSSIA GOODS.

By Order of the Executors to the Will of the Honourable
JOHN BROWN, Efq; deceafed,
On Thurfday the 15th of December next, at the Stores on India-Point, will be Sold, at public Auction (without Referve) the entire Cargo of the Ship *General Wafhington*, *William Smith*, Mafter, from Ruffia, confifting of

130 Tons of St. Peterfburgh clean Hemp
130 Tons of new Sable Iron
 25 Tons of old Sable Iron
  5 Tons of beft afforted fquare Iron
  2 Tons of Sheet Iron
100 Pieces of Ravens Duck
300 Bolts of beft heavy Duck
  2 beft Down Beds
  2 Half Down Ditto
  6 Feather Beds
  1 Cafk of Ifinglafs
  1 Bale of Tickings
 75 Pieces of beft broad bleeched Fleems
  5 or 6 Tons of Cordage afforted, in Lots to fuit Purchafers
Sales to begin at 9 o'Clock, A. M.   The Conditions will be liberal.

Alfo, at 12 o'Clock on the fame Day, the remarkable fine faftfailing Ship GENERAL WASHINGTON, Burthen 360 Tons per Regifter, but will ftow 600 Tons. She is coppered to her loaded Water-Line, has two Suits of Sails, is well found in every Refpect, and could be put to Sea at very fmall Expence.
HEZEKIAH SABIN, *jun.*
Attorney to the Executors of
John Brown, *Efq*;
Providence, November 20, 1803.

were not found in Europe. Corn, hybridized from wild maize used by the Indians, became an important crop in most colonies. In the South, tobacco farming, which the settlers had also learned of from the Indians, was the basis of the economy, and tobacco exports earned sizable revenues. The Indian, idealized as a noble savage, became the symbol of tobacco shops in London.

The early settlers made most of their own clothing. They also made their own textiles, candles, and soaps. In spite of their inventiveness, there were still some items they couldn't make. To bring in extra money for these few necessities, many had a special trade or small surplus of goods to be sold or bartered.

In eighteenth-century America, profit was to be made from catering to the needs of the commoners rather than to the refined tastes of the carriage trade. The alternative to manufacturing a limited volume of luxury goods for the privileged few was producing goods in volume for wide distribution at the lowest possible price. So, at a time when the best artisans in Europe sought wealthy patrons in London, Amsterdam, and Paris for their elegantly crafted furniture, jewelry, and crystal, the American artisans and craftsmen kept their eyes on the needs of their struggling neighbors, whose patronage alone could earn them a profit.

Throughout the colonies, hundreds of part-time inventors and tinkerers were fiddling with contraptions that would improve manufacturing. Eli Whitney, the inventor of the cotton gin, designed an assembly-line process in 1798 to produce muskets for the United States Army. Instead of hiring skilled artisans to make one gun at a time, he hired carpenters to turn out wooden stocks while other workers made barrels or firing apparatuses and assembled the muskets. It was Whitney, not Henry Ford, who first successfully applied the assembly-line process in America.

The ability to provide a larger volume of goods at a lower cost was initially a mixed blessing. In America in the early eighteenth century, customers for manufactured goods were spread over several hundred thousand square miles of rugged terrain, divided by mountains and isolated by poor or nonexistent roads. The challenge to the new manufacturers was to get their products to this widely dispersed populace. In contrast, European families lived in the same place for generations, often maintaining the same standard of living. Tradesmen served the children and grandchildren of families their fathers and grandfathers had served. Communities were self-contained. In some instances, the craft guilds provided a monopoly for local artisans by restricting the territory in which their competitors could work.

In America, the population was expanding, highly

London trade sign for American tobacco. Wooden sign, c. 1675. Private collection.

mobile, and intensely interested in improving its living standard. In fact, the needs of the new communities greatly exceeded what the local artisans and tradesmen could provide. Unlike Europe, America had no restrictive guilds. As a result, artisans and manufacturers envisioned wide distribution for their products. Two Connecticut tinsmiths, Edward and William Pattison, were the first of that typically American species, the Yankee peddler. They were the only tinsmiths in an area where there was consistent demand for their wares, and they aggressively sought customers. Initially, one of the brothers would pack a load of tinware on his back and call on all the homes in the neighborhood. By 1776, they were covering fifteen-hundred-mile routes.

As manufacturers continued to produce an ever wider variety of salable products, peddling became an occupation separate from manufacturing. Peddlers went out for weeks at a time, either on foot with a heavy trunk on their backs or with a horse-drawn wagon loaded with tinware, buttons, thread, dishes, pans, ribbons, and many other items. For several generations in the late eighteenth and early nineteenth centuries, these migratory merchants were the principal distributors to different parts of the country. Housewives looked forward to the peddler's arrival to replenish their supply of small household articles. The peddler was a fount of information about new products that were constantly being turned out by the factories back East. His news and stories of big city life were eagerly awaited by his customers. In the South, peddlers made their way up and down the rivers and bayous in canoes, blowing a conch shell or bugle to call their customers from the plantation mansions and shanties along the banks. Soon peddlers

9

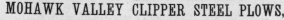
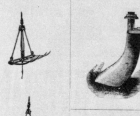

Remington Agricultural Works. Broad-
side. c. 1865. Collection of Business
Americana, Smithsonian Institution.

10

began to buy their own stock instead of acting as agents for manufacturers or taking goods on consignment.

During this early phase of American commerce, hand-made merchandise was not of uniform quality and the customer had to examine what he was buying. Goods were sold through personal contact, and their quality was guaranteed by the seller. In the course of time, brand names were used to set standards of quality.

The Terry clock, manufactured by Eli Terry of Connecticut, is an early example of a brand-name product. Terry had learned the assembly-line process from Eli Whitney. He would pack up his clocks and go out on extended selling trips. To allay his customers' fears that the clocks might not continue ticking after he departed, Terry agreed to collect his money on the next trip. If the clock failed to function, the customer didn't have to pay. But it was a rare individual who didn't pay the next time Terry came around.

The "free-trial" was only one of Terry's sales approaches.

Store poster for Asa Walker, tailor, c. 1840. Baker Library, Harvard University.

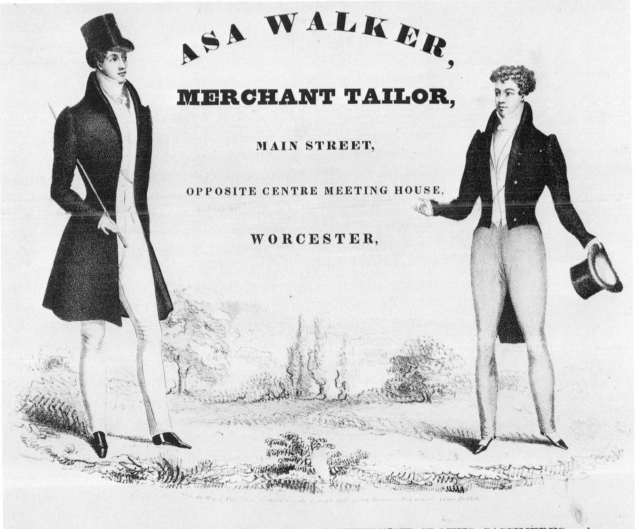

ASA WALKER,

MERCHANT TAILOR,

MAIN STREET,

OPPOSITE CENTRE MEETING HOUSE,

WORCESTER,

KEEPS constantly on hand, an elegant assortment of SUPERFINE CLOTHS, CASSIMERES, and VESTINGS, in all their varieties of Color and Shade; which will be made to order in the best manner, and on the most reasonable terms.

Also, a General Assortment of READY-MADE GARMENTS.

11

Realizing that many people who liked his clocks lacked the means to pay for them in a lump sum, he would accept a small down payment and arrange to collect installments on subsequent visits. This was the beginning of installment buying. Through the combination of an assembly-line process, by which he could produce clocks more cheaply than his competitors could, and a novel sales plan that made his clocks accessible to anyone who wanted one, Eli Terry sold an enormous quantity and was able to cut his price to one-fifth of the original cost within five years. Terry marked each clock with his own name. Its reputation for reliability spread by word of mouth and soon people were willing to buy a Terry clock from a peddler, based on Terry's reputation.

The assembly-line methods of Whitney, Terry, and others accelerated the transition from household industries to factories. Small factories were in operation as early as 1789, when Samuel Slater opened the first cotton mill. Soon factories were producing more than could be sold in their immediate surroundings. The development of improved means of transportation made it possible to distribute goods to a wider market. By 1750, Conestoga wagons were transporting goods throughout the colonies. After the Revolutionary War, they became the primary means of carrying goods westward across the Alleghenies. Eventually they carried passengers and freight to the Pacific Coast. But the early roads were in poor condition and the capacity of the Conestoga wagon was limited.

In time, the steamboat replaced the Conestoga wagon as the cheapest and most efficient means of transporting merchandise. The opening of the Erie Canal in 1825 further increased the opportunity for westward transport at a reasonable rate. The canal became the main artery of passenger and freight traffic between the Northeast and the newly settled territories of the West. Within ten years of the canal's opening, short railroad lines began to spring up along the Eastern Seaboard and, by the mid-1840s, they were providing stiff competition to the steamboats and canal barges.

These means of transportation made it increasingly efficient and inexpensive to ship goods from the Eastern Seaboard to the new settlements across the Alleghenies. The peddler, knowing that he could rely on a steady stream of merchandise from the East, found it more profitable to settle in one place and open a store. Those stores were preceeded by, and continued to get competition from, the flatboats, or "arks," that plied the Ohio, Mississippi, and other western rivers. They were like floating stores with shelves and counters stocked with groceries, hardware, notions, and liquors. Their owners peddled these goods at plantations, villages, and hamlets along the waterways.

12

Where can I buy it?

in every Grocery.

Champion American Soap Powder.
Poster, c. 1860. Library of Congress.

By 1820, local merchants were far more common in the Midwest than were itinerant peddlers. The country store was usually the hub of life in the midwestern and western settlements, and its proprietor found himself in the thick of the town's commercial and personal affairs. The early merchant was aptly described by John Beauchamp Jones in 1849 in the preface to his book, *The Western Merchant:*

He is a general locum tenens, the agent of everybody! And familiar with every transaction in his neighborhood. He is a counselor without license; and yet invariably consulted, not only in matters of business, but in domestic affairs. Parents asked his opinion before giving their consent to their daughters' marriages; and he is always invited to the weddings. He furnishes the nuptial garments for both bride and groom, and his taste is both consulted and adopted. Every item of news, not only local, but from a distance,—as he is frequently the postmaster and the only subscriber to the newspaper—has general dissemination from his establishment, as from a common center; and thither all resort, at least once a week, both for goods and for intelligence.

The general store was simultaneously a grocery, hardware store, pharmacy, and dry-goods emporium. In this sense, it was more diverse than the larger urban department stores, such as A. T. Stewart's in New York, which were opening around the same time. The country merchant, with his varied stock, freed the local residents from producing everything themselves or spending endless hours searching out special items from itinerant peddlers.

The merchant would make one or two trips a year to the big wholesale centers of New York, Boston, Philadelphia, and Baltimore. These commercial centers attracted not only eastern merchants but midwestern store owners as well. Merchants in the Far West visited wholesalers in Kansas City, St. Louis, Chicago, and St. Paul. Transportation was slow, and a buying trip could take as long as six weeks.

Goods arrived from the East Coast in boxes and barrels. Coffee, tea, sugar, flour, and other staples were sold by weight and meted out in containers that customers brought themselves. Coffee was frequently purchased green and roasted by the customer; it was probably kept in small kegs, as was tea. A few standard tea brands like Imperial and Young Hyson dominated the field, although a trade name did not guarantee uniform quality. Brown sugar could be found in open barrels and was frequently sold more readily than the expensive white variety. Soap, spices, flour, and salt completed the stock of staples at an average store. Merchants bought these staples from wholesale grocery houses, and the quality varied from excellent to terrible.

When the country stores first became popular, people still made most of their own clothes. The stores carried bolts of cloth as well as specialty items such as bonnets, gloves, and hosiery. Axes, kettles, pots, and pans crowded the floor along with shoes, saddles, harnesses, and a bewildering variety of other goods. The drug supply included patent medicines and sedatives. Whereas advertising was frequently left to the local merchant, patent medicines, among the earliest products to be advertised, were an exception. In fact, patent medicine advertising, placed by the manufacturer of the product, frequently comprised the majority of a local newspaper's pages. By 1906, advertising claims of patent medicine manufacturers were so exaggerated and flamboyant that, to protect the public, Congress passed the Food and Drug Act.

Color lithographed posters brought back from buying trips in the wholesale centers in the East were hung in store windows or were attached to the glass panels on the entrance doors. Merchants also displayed woodcut posters for farm tools and machinery, which were sent to them by the manufacturers.

The first illustrated posters, like the newspapers, had used stock printer's cuts, but in time wood engravers were commissioned to make special poster illustrations. Early posters announced the departures of steamboats and stagecoaches. Posters were also used in the burgeoning cities in the 1830s and 1840s to publicize the wares of local merchants: musical instruments, elegant clothes, and tobacco.

An innovation of P. T. Barnum, part of his flamboyant

publicity campaign for his American Museum in New York, was the larger-than-life display poster. Before Barnum, woodcut portraits of actors and actresses with heads a mere six inches high had been tacked on walls to advertise plays. Barnum ordered his printer to cut a portrait of himself four times larger than any previously made. Boxwood then used for woodcuts could not be pieced together in a size larger than one foot. Therefore, Barnum's artist chose pine instead. Barnum's three-foot-high head received wide attention wherever it was posted. The portrait was tinted flesh color and became one of the first outdoor posters in color. Barnum led the way in using illustrations in posters: his huge head was followed by pictures of wild animals and other circus attractions. The colorful and appealing circus posters influenced theater bills, which began to show actors in performance rather than just their portraits. By the mid-1860s, circus posters had stimulated the outdoor promotion of other kinds of entertainment, particularly the minstrel troupe and the Wild West Show.

In the early years of the nineteenth century, bartering was still a primary means for the exchange of goods. When cash was paid, the price was determined by the local merchants. If the customer wasn't satisfied with the price, he could bargain for a reduction. A. T. Stewart, who opened a dry-goods store in New York in 1825, was the first merchant to establish a fixed-price policy. His competitors thought he would soon go broke, but Stewart's department store quickly became the largest in the country. Many other retailers adopted his price system, as did most wholesalers and manufacturers. Nonetheless, Stewart was more practical than other merchants both in his selection of clerks and his choice of stock, and the contrast between shopping at his store and others was obvious to many. He was so successful that by 1838 he was able to construct a huge five-story emporium. In 1852, Stewart built the largest department store in the world, a six-story structure that occupied an entire square block and employed more than two thousand people. Stewart then became one of the richest men in America.

R. H. Macy, who started a small retail dry-goods store in Haverhill, Massachusetts, in 1851, went a step beyond Stewart. At a time when merchants extended generous credit terms to their customers, Macy accepted cash only. By maintaining a steady cash flow, he contended that his prices could be lower than those of his competitors. In 1857, Macy left Haverhill and opened a small store in New York, where his policy of buying and selling for cash and underselling the competition made him an immediate success. He continued to add new lines of merchandise until his store grew to be one of the largest in the city.

THE MASTODON
AIR-TIGHT COOKING RANGE,

FOR
LONG
WOOD.

OR

COAL.

The undersigned has the pleasure of offering to the public, a Cooking Range, which he confidently believes overcomes all objections to other Ranges, and upon trial will prove to be the most economical, convenient and comfortable Range extant It is fitted to burn long wood or coal, and being upon the Air-Tight principle, and from the peculiar construction of the flues can be used at about two-thirds the expense of other Ranges. The large sizes for Hotels, Restorators, Steamboats, Hospitals, &c. contain FOURTEEN BOILERS and FOUR OVENS. The small sizes for families contain SIX BOILERS and THREE OVENS. By using wood in Summer, and closing the dampers between meals, it will not make the room uncomfortably warm; while in Winter it will warm the room as well as other ranges with much less consumption of coal. The ovens are all in front, avoiding the danger and inconvenience of reaching over the fire to use them, and the main oven being elevated prevents the inconvenience of stooping.

In Winter, the food can be easily kept warm by the auxiliary ovens and large surface. The flues can be cleaned when foul, in a few minutes *without taking out the oven*, and if the iron work should require repairs, it can be taken apart, and replaced *without disturbing the brick work.*

References can be given where these Ranges are in use, and one can be seen ready for operation at the RANGE AND FURNACE WAREHOUSE, No. 25 Devonshire street, Boston.

☞Hot Air Furnaces for warming Churches, Houses, Stores, &c.

Upon the most improved, econonomical and compact models.

☞**Cooking, Air-Tight, Parlor, Hall and Chamber Stoves and Pipe; Oven and Ash Pit Doors; Coal Hole Covers; Portable Wash Boilers; Portable Furnaces; Copper, Tin and Sheet-Iron Wares kept for sale and manufactured to order.**

PROFESSOR MOTT'S PATENT PREMIUM VENTILATOR AND SMOKE BLOWER.
SEALED WEIGHTS AND MEASURES.

JOHN M. DEARBORN,
NO. 25 DEVONSHIRE STREET.

Boston, September, 1847.

J. G. Torrey, printer, No. 23 Devonshire Street, Boston.

Mastodon Air-Tight Cooking Range. Woodcut poster. c. 1847. Baker Library, Harvard University.

A. T. Stewart's and Macy's were the first two department stores in the United States. The reforms in pricing and selling that they inaugurated were instrumental in the move toward the sale of brand-name goods at a uniform price throughout the nation.

As cities grew, more and more people left rural areas to work in the factories and offices. These workers became part of a new middle class with cash to spend and increasingly sophisticated tastes.

Along with greater disposable income came the demand for more comforts. The transition from wood to coal made cooking ranges more efficient and particularly desirable in cities, where firewood was less accessible than it was in rural areas. Some ranges, like the Mastodon Air-Tight cooking range, could burn coal in the winter and wood in the summer. In the 1850s, Shepard Chapin & Company marketed a parlor stove that could also be used for baking. Early refrigerators, called iceboxes, were insulated containers for the blocks of ice delivered daily by an iceman. Gas and electric refrigerators were not introduced until the 1920s.

In 1836 there were only fifteen hundred bathtubs in the United States, all of them in Philadelphia, which had a city water system and levied a three-dollar tax on each tub. Until well into the nineteenth century, many physicians considered frequent bathing inadvisable. Before the Civil War, luxury taxes on tubs, taxes on water, and a lack of adequate plumbing militated against the bathtub. Even when decent water pressure was available, few middle class people thought of installing a tub. As late as the 1870s, bathrooms were considered luxuries reserved for the wealthy. E. J. Knowlton of Ann Arbor, Michigan, was selling a movable tub, which he claimed was "more convenient than a stationary bathtub with no expense of bathroom and fixtures." By the late 1800s, builders of moderately priced apartments had begun to install zinc-lined bathtubs in addition to indoor plumbing.

City dwellers, dependent on others for food, clothing, and general needs, became the primary customers for ready-made goods and brand-name products. They were also the principal consumers of produce from rural areas. The expansion of agriculture to provide food for the urban centers was made possible by the improvement of farming methods and the invention of better tools and labor-saving machinery. By 1830, factories produced thousands of farm implements a year. The McCormick reaper, patented in 1834, was instrumental in the development of large-scale agriculture, which in turn meant the production of more food by fewer people. At the London World's Fair in 1851, the London *Times* called McCormick's reaper "a cross

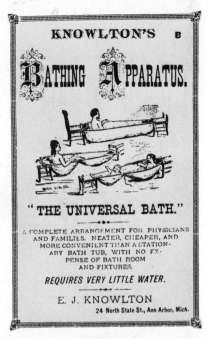

Knowlton's Bathing Apparatus. Poster, c. 1860. Collection of Business Americana, Smithsonian Institution.

McCormick Reaper. Poster made from a photograph, c. 1860. Collection of Business Americana, Smithsonian Institution. The McCormick Reaper, drawn by two camels, helped Asiatic Russia harvest wheat as early as 1860. McCormick, Howe, John Deere, and International Harvester farm equipment was exported all over the world.

between Astley's chariot and a flying machine"; but sentiment changed after it was demonstrated.

By midcentury, there was already a sizable demand for ready-made garments, although business did not become respectable until after the Civil War. The ready-made clothing business was started by secondhand clothing dealers, who sold piles of patched and worn garmets to seamen. When demand exceeded supply, some dealers went into manufacturing. Since most of their customers sailed off to distant ports after purchasing their wares, they felt no obligation to produce quality merchandise. They bought defective cloth, paid tailors a low rate to design the patterns, and established a cottage industry with most of the sewing being done in farm homes. The frustrated customers were at sea in more ways than one. Their elbows soon poked through the jacket sleeves and their pants shrank. During this early period of clothing manufacture, A. T. Stewart refused to sell this kind of shoddy merchandise. He advertised that his store carried "everything but men's and boy's ready-made clothing."

The widespread sale of poor quality goods prompted reforms in the clothing industry that were paralleled by reforms in the manufacturing and merchandising of food, although food products were among the last to be improved. In New York, it was common for granulated sugar to be mixed with pounded rice. Pepper might be mixed with dust. Cocoa was commonly adulterated with brown clay mixed with mutton fat to give it the correct oily consistency. Likewise, the dried leaves of trees and shrubs were added to tea. These underhanded practices continued until foods were packaged and sold under an advertised brand name with the reputation of the manufacturer as a guarantee of quality.

Before national brand names were introduced, goods were preserved and packed in various kinds of containers for transport by wagon, boat, and train over the long distances that separated producers from their markets. Flour was shipped in cotton sacks until after the Civil War when a sturdy paper bag was perfected. Other goods were shipped in cumbersome wooden boxes before the invention of the cardboard carton.

Early on, manufacturers pictured packages of their goods on their posters. A poster for Preston & Merrill showed the multitudinous products of the company all lined up in their bottles and boxes. This was an ideal way for the company to impress the consumer not only with the variety of goods it manufactured but with the packages themselves. As packages for products became prevalent, poster artists began to develop the idea that products could be made more desirable if held by someone. Later, packages were identified

Premium Plough. Woodcut poster, c. 1840. Chicago Historical Society.

with a well-known figure like Uncle Sam, as in a Wheatlet poster of 1899. Packages on nineteenth-century advertising posters prefigured their later widespread use in magazine advertisements. Richard B. Franken and Carroll B. Larabee observed in their 1928 book, *Packages That Sell*, that in 1900 only 7 percent of a sample study of large-circulation general magazine advertisements showed a picture of the package, but by 1925 this had increased to 35 percent and was still climbing.

In 1810, a Parisian chef won a prize for inventing a practical method of preserving cooked foods by sealing them in glass jars at boiling point temperature. The preservation of food in tin cans was a variant of this idea. Canning did not begin to flourish in the United States until 1874, but with the perfection of the canning process and the invention of machinery to produce cheaper and better cans, the multibillion-dollar processed food industry was launched.

Packing eventually became packaging, which was intended to sell the product as well as preserve it. Before the package could become an effective selling tool, however, a number of other elements had to fall into place. This occurred early in the twentieth century when the mass-production process, the container, the chain stores, and national advertising coalesced into a system of marketing that is, in itself, one of the significant inventions of modern commerce.

CHAPTER TWO
WILD CLAIMS AND BRAND NAMES: 1865-1900

The Civil War, with its great demand for supplies and equipment, was an important stimulus to American manufacturing in the 1860s. Before the war, most goods were either made in limited quantities by small manufacturing industries or they were made at home. Wartime manufacturing ushered in the era of mass production. Many cotton factories were converted into woolen mills to provide the fabric for uniforms, undergarments, blankets, and coats. The increase in the production of quality woolen cloth for wartime use ensured that such fabric would be available after the war.

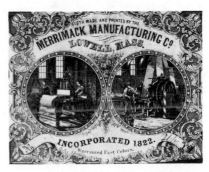

Merrimack Manufacturing Company. Poster, c. 1850. Collection of Business Americana, Smithsonian Institution. Label from a bolt of cloth.

The sewing machine, which Elias Howe had put on the market in 1849, was vital to the mass production of clothing. During the war, sewing machines were adapted for use in factories where footwear, harnesses, saddles, and clothing were produced in quantity. The discovery that certain sets of body measurements occurred with regularity was a revelation for the ready-made clothing industry and an essential piece of knowledge for the rapid manufacture of army uniforms. When the war was over, the measurements were available to manufacturers of civilian clothing, who began to supply ready-made garments to an unprecedented market. Less than half of all men's clothing sold in 1880 was ready-made, but it was the rare individual who didn't wear ready-made garments by the beginning of the twentieth century.

John Wanamaker, who started as a young tailor in

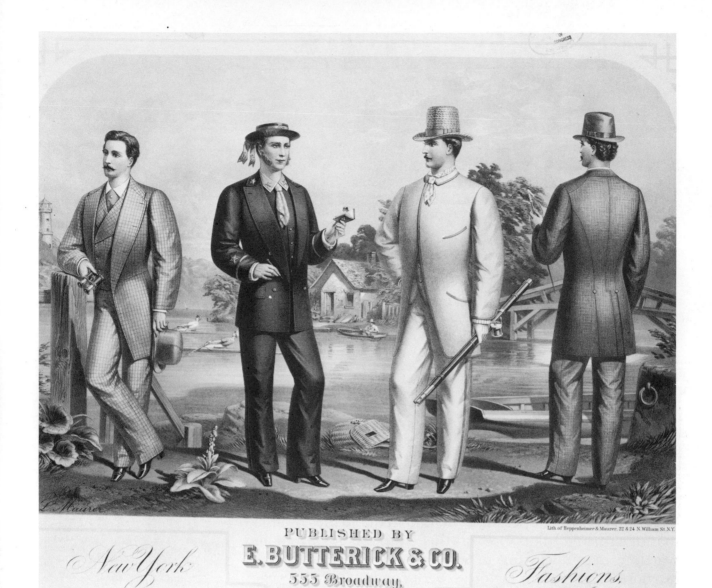

PUBLISHED BY
E. BUTTERICK & CO.
555 Broadway,

New York   Fashions,

Lith. of Heppenheimer & Maurer, 22 & 24 N. William St. N.Y.

Butterick & Company. Poster, c. 1874. Metropolitan Museum of Art. Prior to the availability of ready-made clothes, fashions were determined by pattern manufacturers who visited European capitals and brought back styles for American use.

Philadelphia in 1837, made the ready-made clothing business respectable. By 1869, he had built a department store in Philadelphia to rival A. T. Stewart's and Macy's in New York. His suits cost a good deal more than those of his competitors, but they were cheaper than the elegant clothes made by custom tailors. The lower price for quality clothing was a major factor in eliminating the visible signs of class that had previously distinguished the wealthy entrepreneur from the small merchant. Wanamaker's policy of selling quality merchandise at a lower price was such a success that by 1874 he had become the largest retail merchandiser in the United States, despite the fact that he sold nothing but men's and boy's clothing and furnishings.

The increase in ready-made pants and coats stimulated the production of other ready-to-wear items. Production of men's shirts, collars, and cuffs had begun as early as 1820. Separate washable collars resulted in a demand for cleanliness that the most skilled laundresses would have difficulty achieving. For a time paper collars were popular. These

from preoccupation with its own survival and opened the way to a more comfortable life. Predominant among those who embraced the values of the emerging consumer culture were immigrants who poured into America—particularly the cities—from the 1880s on. Many envisioned the United States as an El Dorado where they could make their fortunes. They saw in the acquisition of goods and wealth a way of pulling themselves up the social ladder not available to them in Europe, where class was defined by birth rather than by material possessions.

Social critics pointed out, however, that the relentless pursuit of comforts and conveniences that characterized the emergent middle class was a debasement of the higher ideals on which America had been founded. One of the harshest critics of America's material values was Thorstein Veblen, whose *The Theory of the Leisure Class* appeared in 1899. Veblen was a self-styled radical who challenged the relentless quest for prestige and self-esteem that was signified by the acquisition of goods. At the time Veblen's book appeared, Americans had too much of a stake in their country's growing economy to take him seriously. It wasn't until the hard times hit after the stock market crash of 1929 that his ideas on conspicuous consumption and conspicuous waste caused the Depression generation to rethink its values.

The period between the end of the Civil War and the turn of the century, which Mark Twain called the 'Gilded Age, was one of phenomenal growth. America's industrial progress was marked by the 1876 Centennial Exhibition in Philadelphia, which followed by twenty-five years Britain's Crystal Palace Exhibition, the first official display of the products of the Industrial Revolution.

Visitors to the centennial were treated to a dazzling show of American mechanical ingenuity. Alexander Graham Bell, a young Scottish phonetics teacher, demonstrated his newly patented telephone. The colossal steam engine invented by Henry Corliss was one of the main attractions, with its twin vertical cylinders as imposing as the columns of an Egyptian temple. The engine was so powerful that it could run all the machinery in the building that housed it. Manufacturers, quick to capitalize on the excitement generated by the centennial, issued posters linking bock beer, cooking ranges, and other products with the celebration of American's first hundred years.

Between 1860 and 1869, the United States Patent Office granted 77,355 patents. By 1899, this number had jumped to 234,749. Notable among the many inventions that had an impact on social change and economic development were barbed wire (1874), which made possible the cheap and efficient fencing of vast areas of land for cattle

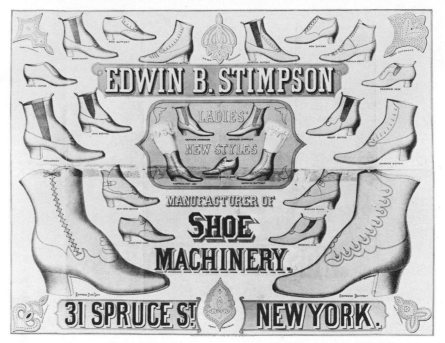

Edwin B. Stimpson. Poster, c. 1879. Baker Library, Harvard University. This sewing machine manufacturer decided to show the end product, a "crooked shoe," rather than the machine itself; a progressive idea for the 19th century.

were followed by celluloid ones, which men wore well into the twentieth century.

Nineteenth-century women wore long skirts that swept the streets and shirtwaists with high collars. Standards of beauty called for women to look delicate at the expense of comfort. Beneath their flowing skirts and billowing shirts, they wore tightly laced corsets in an attempt to make their waists small enough to be encircled by two hands. Physicians and women's rights advocates opposed this practice but made little headway. Women often wore shoes a size too small as well. Besides the corsets, they wore layers of chemises, drawers, corset covers, and several petticoats. Huge hats were perched on full heads of hair, girded by an array of hatpins, hairpins, haircombs, and often false hair. Such fashions were intended to reinforce a woman's social role. Women had been trained to sacrifice their comfort and independence to a social ideal that confined them to looking fragile, minding the children, and serving the wishes of their husbands. They were imprisoned in this role in economic as well as social terms by exclusion from decent jobs until they were of necessity drawn into the labor force beginning with the Civil War.

Sometimes a change in fashion depended on the invention of a new piece of machinery. Until the mid-nineteenth century, ready-made shoes were called "straights"; there was no difference between the right and left shoe. Manufacturers remedied this deficiency with the "crooked shoe," cut to distinguish between the right and left foot. The revolution in the production of footwear came with the invention of the McKay machine for sewing soles to uppers. It was introduced in 1862, just in time to meet the Union

army's demand for thousands of pairs of shoes. After the war, factory-made shoes were first produced for the working class. The middle class and the well-to-do, who were more finicky in their taste, had to wait another twenty years for a quality manufactured shoe to their liking.

As the manufacture of all kinds of equipment in large quantities increased, the need for standardized mechanical parts arose. The use of interchangeable parts, pioneered by Eli Whitney in 1798 with the assembly-line manufacture of muskets, came to be known as the "American system." During the Civil War, the need for large quantities of military goods coupled with the shortage of labor provided the impetus needed to advance this system. The result was the standardized production of clothing, shoes, harnesses, and tents, as well as many other items.

The Civil War also brought about great changes in the labor force and ultimately in consumer habits. With most of the men at the front, women filled the vacant factory jobs and had to do the men's work on the farms. Household articles that they had previously made themselves were now purchased with their wartime wages. Customarily, the man had handled the finances of the household; now it was the woman who did the buying. Canned and packaged foods became staples since working women had less time for the lengthy preparation of meals. Those who lived in the cities couldn't produce any food themselves and had to depend on the local grocer for their needs.

The first canned food to be nationally advertised was soup. H. J. Heinz, one of the bolder advertisers of the late nineteenth century, was the man who made canned foods a part of the culture. He conceived the idea of "57 Varieties" while riding a train from Pittsburgh to New York. Soon his slogan was conspicuous on cliffsides and building walls everywhere. In the 1890s, streetcar signs advertising Heinz Oven-Baked beans used an actual string of dried beans, which rattled as the streetcar bounced over the tracks.

Packaged breakfast cereals first became popular in the 1870s. Hornby's oatmeal and Quaker oats had extensive campaigns to advertise their products. Hornby's trademark showed Oliver Twist getting a bowl of porridge from the school cook and saying, "I want some more."

Joseph Priestley, an English chemist, was indirectly responsible for America's most refreshing beverage, soda pop. Priestley discovered that the bubbling water of an English spa was simply H_2O with carbon dioxide in it. But it was a Philadelphian named North who invented an apparatus for making carbonated water, which could be drunk as plain soda water or mixed with a variety of sweet, sticky syrups. Charles G. Hires discovered the formula for his root beer syrup in the 1870s and led the way in

advertising "soft drinks." Coca-Cola, which dates initially offered free samples by advertising with that read "Good for a Coca-Cola for you and yo Within five years, a plethora of small Coca-Co signs, and decals were in evidence everywhere. Coca-Cola syrup was mixed with soda water and a glass. Later, the drink was bottled. An early post bottled product pointed out that it was made fron ated water and called it, with Barnumesque hyperb Most Refreshing Drink in the World."

The soft drink was a welcome alternative to w those who disdained beer, wine, and spirits. In America, however, most people preferred fermented The lower classes drank beer; the aristocrats, peach or gin, at first, then rum or whiskey; and those middle consumed beer and wine.

Colonial brewers, less sophisticated than their terparts in Europe, added spruce twigs, birch bark, pu kin or apple parings to their beer instead of difficult-t hops. With the migration of many Germans to the Un States, beginning early in the nineteenth century, brew became more sophisticated. Lager beer, a German specia could be made in America only with yeast imported fr Europe. Breweries such as those of Joseph Schlitz a Anheuser-Busch were established in cities with large Ge man populations—Cincinnati, Milwaukee, and St. Loui Eventually, stiff competition led to the consolidation smaller breweries into a few giant concerns. Desperate fo distribution outlets, the smaller breweries set up chains of saloons where only their own brands were sold. Opponents of the saloons formed the Anti-Saloon League, which, in the 1890s, embarked on a campaign and eventually succeeded in closing the drinking establishments.

During colonial times, wine was an expensive import and remained so for many years. Early American contributions to the multitude of alcoholic beverages were rye whiskey and corn whiskey, later known as bourbon. Scotch-Irish immigrants had brought their pot-stills with them. With these, they turned the American crop of rye and corn into a liquid that could easily be transported. The presence of liquor-making equipment in Appalachia and the Pacific Northwest accounted for whiskey's replacing the Eastern Seaboard's rum and peach brandy as the favored American thirst quencher. People with scruples imbibed their liquor in the form of medication. One type of medicinal compound, known as "bitters," contained rye or bourbon as its principal ingredient. The advertising for bitters and tonics promised relief from coughs, colds, consumption, and other maladies.

The plethora of ready-made clothing, canned and packaged edibles, and laborsaving devices liberated the family

grazing in the West; and the incandescent lamp (1879) and the phonograph (1877), both the work of Thomas Edison. The trolley car, automobile, cash register, electric furnace, and steam turbine were others in the bewildering array of inventions produced during this period.

In the latter part of the nineteenth century, a railroad boom made it possible to ship freight from one coast to the other at a low cost. Farsighted merchants were quick to see the implications that low-cost rail transportation had for merchandising. Their response was the chain store. One of the first chains was started by George Huntington Hartford, who, in 1859, imported a shipment of tea from China and sold it on a New York dock for one-third the price retail stores were charging. The idea of buying directly from Asia, bypassing the middlemen, and selling at a small markup proved successful. Instead of selling on the docks, Hartford decided to open a store, which he called the Great Atlantic Tea Company. As business increased, he opened more stores in New York City and expanded to Boston and Philadelphia. By 1880, his firm was called the Great Atlantic and Pacific Tea Company, soon shortened to A&P, and a chain of ninety-five stores stretched from Milwaukee to Boston. By 1912, there were five hundred stores.

The railroad was the key factor in the success of the A&P. National merchandising would not have been possible without a network of rail lines for shipping merchandise from central locations at a price far lower than it had previously cost to send it by barge or Conestoga wagon.

Another man who understood the advantage of low-cost rail distribution was Frank Woolworth, who observed while clerking in a dry-goods store that customers who ordinarily would ask for credit had no hesitation about paying cash for odds and ends selling at five and ten cents each. After several failures, Woolworth opened a successful store which stocked no merchandise costing more than a dime. By 1895, he had a chain of twenty-five stores and continued to expand.

J. C. Penney was an entrepreneur who saw the potential of a chain of "working man's" department stores. The Wanamakers, the Macys, and the Marshall Fields had higher-priced goods for city people, so Penney took his merchandise to the smaller towns where his Golden Rule Stores sometimes had the local saloon for a neighbor.

While city and town dwellers were shopping at the A&P, Woolworth's, and Golden Rule Stores, country folks were limited to the few items their local merchant could import from the cities. Aaron Montgomery Ward's response to this was to sell through the mail. As a traveling salesman for a dry-goods manufacturer just after the Civil War, Ward got to know the farmers and the limitations of the general

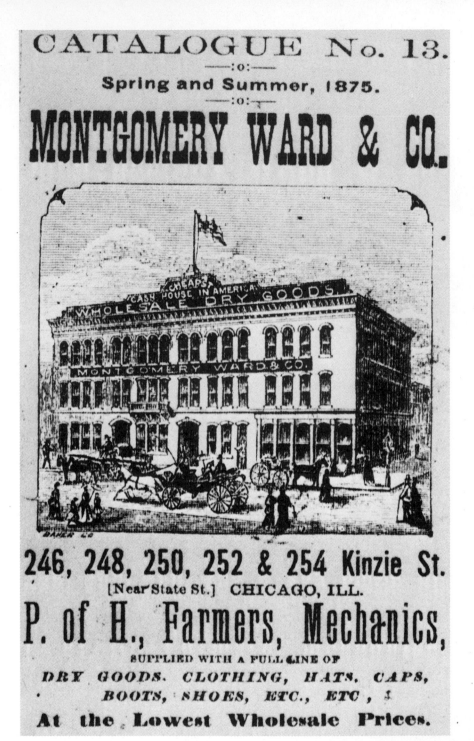

CATALOGUE No. 13.
—:o:—
Spring and Summer, 1875.
—:o:—
MONTGOMERY WARD & CO.

246, 248, 250, 252 & 254 Kinzie St.
[Near State St.] CHICAGO, ILL.
P. of H., Farmers, Mechanics,
SUPPLIED WITH A FULL LINE OF
DRY GOODS, CLOTHING, HATS, CAPS,
BOOTS, SHOES, ETC., ETC., ¡
At the Lowest Wholesale Prices.

stores. Ward saw that he could lower retail prices by selling directly to rural customers. He started a mail-order business in Chicago in 1872 by issuing a single sheet listing items for sale along with instructions for ordering. Within two years, the single sheet had become a seventy-two-page catalog. By eliminating the middleman, Ward saved his customers 40 percent. In 1884 the catalog listed nearly ten thousand items generously illustrated with small wood cuts, adaptations of posters, showing the items for sale. The purchaser's risk was reduced by Ward's guarantee that any item found unsatisfactory could be returned.

28

Ward was soon rivaled by another Chicago mail-order business, Sears, Roebuck and Company. Richard Warren Sears managed to build a wide following with such homilies as "Satisfaction Guaranteed or Your Money Back" and claims that his goods were "The Best in the World." Sears concluded that if the catalog had replaced the salesperson in representing the product, then it ought to be lavishly printed to make the products more attractive. In 1903, he set up his own printing plant and eventually was producing beautifully illustrated and superbly printed color catalogs.

National manufacturers, who began slowly after the Civil War and grew rapidly after the 1880s, had to sell their products to customers whom they would never meet. Without the opportunity to make a personal sales pitch, the manufacturer sought other ways to attract the customer. One was the employment of an advertising specialist. Although advertising didn't become widespread until the 1890s, the first agency was set up by Volney Palmer in Philadelphia in 1841. Initially, the advertising agent's job was to solicit advertising for the newspapers, who paid him a commission. Another advertising pioneer, George P. Rowell, went a step beyond that. He made enormous profits by purchasing advertising space in large quantities from country weeklies and selling it in smaller parcels to advertisers at a retail price. Although advertisers paid fixed amounts for the newspaper circulation of their ads, they had no idea how many people they were reaching until Rowell compiled the first edition of the *American Newspaper Directory*, which he published in 1869. This volume was the first attempt to list all the newspapers of the United States with an accurate estimate of their circulations.

G. P. Rowell & Company's Advertising Agency. Broadside, c. 1860. Collection of Business Americana, Smithsonian Institution.

Around this time, the number of agencies began to increase. To outdo their competition, some offered copywriting as an additional service. Agencies began to specialize. J. Walter Thompson was the first to promote magazine advertising in a big way, and E. C. Allen became an expert in direct-mail selling.

Until the 1890s, copy was written by a separate group of writers called "literary men." Some were employed directly by manufacturers, others were freelancers. Early advertising copy was intended merely to establish the product's identity, but as competition between brands increased extravagant claims were made. Patent medicine manufacturers, among the earliest and most aggressive advertisers, were masters of hyperbolic prose. This promotional style was influenced by P. T. Barnum, whose claim to "The Greatest Show on Earth" inspired some manufacturers to apply superlatives indiscriminately.

In the late 1860s, John Powers introduced "honest copy," a technique he developed through the years while working for Wanamaker's department stores and other advertisers. Powers insisted on telling the literal truth. One day, while Powers was working at Wanamaker's, an employee told him that the store had a load of gossamers—light, waterproof raincoats—to sell. Powers' ad the next day stated precisely, "We have a lot of rotten gossamers and things we want to get rid of." The raincoats were sold out the same morning. Despite this, Powers' honesty was too much for John Wanamaker, who eventually fired him. Powers became a successful freelance copywriter for Carter's Little Liver Pills, Macbeth Lamp Chimneys, and Murphy's varnish. His terse evocative statements, known as the "Powers style," were years ahead of their time.

The manufacturers of Sapolio, the laundry soap, took a different tack. They hired a young copywriter named Bret Harte, author of *The Luck of Roaring Camp,* to write verses to accompany the humorous illustrations they favored. Harte's first series of verses helped inaugurate the jingle craze in the mid-1870s. Perhaps he had Longfellow's "Excelsior" in mind when he wrote under a picture of mountain wilderness:

> One Sabbath morn, as heavenward
> White Mountain tourists slowly spurred
> On every rock, to their dismay
> That read that legend, always
> USE SAPOLIO

According to an 1867 article in *The Galaxy,* a small Boston monthly, advertising in the United States was at the point where "the names of successful advertisers have become household words where great poets, politicians, philosophers and warriors of the land are as yet unheard of; there is instant recognition of Higg's saleratus and Wigg's soap even where the title of Tennyson's last work is thought to be 'In a Garden' and Longfellow was understood as the nickname of a tall man."

In spite of the *Galaxy's* optimism, advertising was far from being generally accepted. Many manufacturers in the 1870s and 1880s thought advertising undignified and even disreputable. They didn't see the value of stimulating customer demand before the products reached the store. As far as they were concerned, it was up to the wholesaler and the retailer to create an interest in the product. According to A. D. Lasker, founder of the Lord & Thomas advertising agency, as late as 1898 manufacturers frequently had to hide their advertising expenditures from their bankers, who thought that manufacturers who advertised were unreliable. Only a handful of national manufacturers—Kodak, Royal baking powder, Singer, Steinway, and Sapolio—advertised extensively in the 1870s and 1880s.

Nathaniel Fowler, a prominent copywriter of the 1880s, was known for his Columbia bicycle ads. Fowler took a hard-nosed approach to advertising copy. "All this poppy-cock advertising may look well," he said, "and like the sensational preacher create a tremendous stir, but the question is, 'Does it sell goods?'"

In the 1870s and 1880s, the fact that a high percentage of people did not read newspapers made the poster or outdoor sign a more widely used advertising medium. Even in the early 1890s, 25 percent of all advertising expenditure was still going into outdoor advertising. Short copy on posters and signs had sold goods. Agencies began to adopt the same approach for newspaper and magazine advertisements. "Use Sapolio" and other brief exhortations, set in large type and accompanied by a few lines of text, became the outstanding style of advertising in the early 1890s. Earlier in the century, poster illustrations had stimulated the use of pictures in newspaper advertisements; now posters were influencing copy style as well. In the following decade, one manufacturer after another ventured timidly into advertising. When sales mounted, they became more aggressive, and soon their competitors followed.

By 1900, manufacturers were capable of producing more goods than the public could consume; some means was required to create desires where none previously existed. At this point, advertising was called upon to help create new markets. Agencies began to pull together the talents of the space broker, the copywriter, and the artist. This resulted in the "full-service agency," which could meet all the needs of a client.

The oldest of these agencies was N. W. Ayer & Son, started in 1869 by a father and son who began, as did other agents, by selling newspaper space to advertisers. Their largest clientele was drawn from the patent medicine business. Eventually they graduated to more respectable clients like John Wanamaker, Montgomery Ward, Ferry Seeds, and Singer Sewing Machines. During the boom years of advertising in the latter part of the nineteenth century, Ayer garnered many prestigious accounts: Procter & Gamble, Burpee Seeds, Fairy Soap, and Gold Dust Cleanser were but a few. Despite its increased activities, the Ayer agency still looked upon copywriters as an expensive nuisance and art directors as a luxury. Ayer didn't hire a full-time copywriter until 1892; the first art director joined the firm six years later. Initially, Ayer began selling magazine advertising space when J. Walter Thompson, which had cornered the magazine market, announced that it was selling newspaper space. The agency had likewise frowned on outdoor advertising until pressed into that field by one of its clients in 1898.

TRADE
(William)

MARK
(Andrew)

With the selling of merchandise becoming more impersonal, manufacturers had to devise ways of distinguishing their products from those of their competitors. The trademark was one way to accomplish this. Trademarks were occasionally used in the United States before the Revolutionary War, but there was little stimulus for a wider use until 1866, the year William and Andrew Smith inherited a cough drop business from their father. The success of the medication, sold as Smith Brothers Cough Drops, had inspired a host of competitors to capitalize on their reputation by using such names as Schmitt Brothers or Smith & Bros. that could easily confuse the customer. At the time, a manufacturer still had no legal protection for the name of his product. To protect their interests, the Smiths designed a distinctive trademark: a picture of each of them with the word *Trade* under William's picture and *Mark* under Andrew's. This led stage comedians to refer to the brothers as Trade and Mark Smith. The mark of identification appeared on all the glass jars in which their cough drops were displayed. Still, nothing prevented a druggist from putting a competitor's cough drops in a Smith Brothers jar. The brothers devised a way to protect themselves from *that* deception. In 1872, they packed their cough drops in paper boxes, thus becoming the first firm to distribute its wares in factory-filled packages.

The first trademark registered by the United States Patent Office, on October 25, 1870, was an eagle that represented the Averill Chemical Paint Company of New York. The company's application described it thus:

In the foreground, on a rock, with the word Chemistry upon it is an eagle holding in his mouth a paint-pot or cannister, with a brush, and a ribbon or streamer, on which are the words, Economical, Durable, Beautiful. Below the feet of the bird is represented water, upon which is a steamer and other vessels.

32

GOLD DUST

GOLD DUST

GOLD DUST
THE WORLD'S BEST CLEANSER.

FAIRBANK'S GOLD DUST shing Powder.

Such trademarks were typical of the grandiose metaphors popular in the United States until the 1890s. With the rise of cities and the influx of immigrants, America was becoming the proverbial melting pot. The way people talked about the "American Experience" was increasingly colloquial and rooted in daily life. The trademarks that became identified with products reflected this trend. Instead of allegorical figures, a host of animals, birds, children, and comic types were created by imaginative copywriters and artists to give their clients' products a comfortable familiarity. Some trademarks represented the product's attributes. The droll little woman in wooden shoes who chases dirt with a big stick identified Old Dutch Cleanser and represented its ability to get rid of filth. Likewise, the Gold Dust Twins, the trademark for N. B. Fairbank Company's Gold Dust Washing Powder, scrubbed pots and tubs until they could see their reflections in them. Their immense popularity and sales effectiveness was an indication of white Americans' naive and insensitive attitude toward the portrayal of blacks in the 1890s.

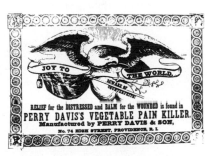

Perry Davis' Vegetable Pain Killer. Poster, c. 1870. Private collection.

The famous Levi Strauss & Company
trademark showing two horses strain-
ing to pull a pair of Levis apart appeared in the 1870s. The word "blue-
jeans" written as one word first
appeared around 1880. Courtesy of
Levi Strauss & Company.

Sweet Orr & Company, the eastern
equivalent of "Levis," made labor history in the 1890s by welcoming union
organizers. Their line of bib-overalls
was manufactured in specific standard sizes, an idea practically unheard of before the twentieth century.

Figures were created to endorse a host of other products.
The benign old Quaker in eighteenth-century dress represented solidity and good sense. People took his words to
heart when he declared, "Those who eat Quaker Oats have
less desire for meat, and they will always tell you that they
feel better." In addition, the fulsome mammy known as
Aunt Jemima signified to purchasers of pancake flour that
their pancakes would have the same down-home goodness
as those that came from her own warm, homey kitchen.
Other trademarks, while less pictorial, indelibly stamped
the images of a bevy of products on the minds of thousands
of consumers.

Trademarks were often coupled with slogans. The
Morton Salt trademark was a little girl with an umbrella

carrying a container of Morton salt under her arm, the salt spilling from its spout. The slogan that went with the picture, "When it rains, it pours," was a claim of the salt's ability to pour even in damp weather without lumping together. Some slogans were attempts to endow products with special qualities. Ivory soap's "99 and 44/100% pure" and Carnation milk's "From Contented Cows" are examples of these.

Trademarks and slogans in the 1890s were usually the inspiration of an individual. They were adopted because the client liked them and not because market research guaranteed their effectiveness, although the huge success of many of them testified to the intuitive hunches of their creators.

The adoption of trademarks was concurrent with the expansion of outdoor advertising. During the Civil War, poster use was stimulated by the United States government, which put up posters to recruit volunteers for the Union army. Before 1870, outdoor advertisements were posted and painted by individuals who were either employed by advertisers or by small local companies in a limited territory. Just after the war, there were more than 275 professional billposting and board- and rock-painting concerns in the United States, each of whom employed from two to twenty men. The first national painting service was organized in 1870 by the firm of Bradbury and Houghteling, which became the leading outdoor advertising company during the next ten years.

"Hote" Houghteling had a reputation for painting signs on rocks that others deemed inaccessible. The firm's major clients were the leading patent medicine manufacturers— St. Jacob's oil, which exceeded all its rivals in the number and size of its advertisements, Tutts Pills, Wizard Oil, and Hoods' Sarsaparilla. The firm also painted signs for tobacco manufacturers—Bull Durham, Battle Ax Plug, and the Official Five Cent Cigar. Several other sign-painting concerns of the period were R. J. Gunning, Thomas Cusak, and O. J. Gude, who was later to be the guiding force behind the proliferation of enormous signs along New York's Broadway.

Before these companies were formed, itinerant sign painters had roamed the countryside propositioning farmers for the use of a side of their barn. The sign painters made various arrangements with the farmers. Most commonly they would paint the entire barn in exchange for the use of one side for an advertising sign. Products ordinarily advertised in this way were patent medicines and tobaccos. Mail Pouch tobacco was advertised regularly on the sides of barns and continues to be today.

Unfortunately, the sign painters didn't stick to barns.

Ferry Seeds. Poster, c. 1890. Private collection. A sign within a poster; a common practice among advertisers in the late nineteenth century.

Duryea's Corn Starch. Trade card, c. 1880. Private collection.

The once-virgin landscape became progressively cluttered with signs painted on walls, posts, trees, and rocks. A trade card of the New York Advertising Sign Company, which advertised "Signs Painted Anywhere," showed an artist sitting on a tightrope painting a sign on Niagara Falls. Patent medicine manufacturers were the greatest despoilers of the landscape. From the 1860s to the 1880s, painted letters from six inches to two feet high advertised home remedies on rocks and cliffs, barns, abandoned structures, and any other available surface.

Outdoor rock painting reached its apotheosis in the huge sign that Bradbury and Houghteling actually painted at Niagara Falls to advertise St. Jacob's Oil. The sign became the talk of the country. So many visitors to the falls criticized it that it was eventually removed. Nonetheless, the words *St. Jacob's Oil* were painted on barns, fences, and trees in thousands of towns across the country. One of the manufacturer's famous stunts was to purchase a Mississippi River steamboat on which St. Jacob's Oil was painted in letters twelve feet high so they could be read from a great distance while the boat delivered cargoes of the elixir up and down the river. The company's trademark, a bearded figure, was shown on a trade card as a new Statue of Liberty, holding aloft a bottle of St. Jacob's Oil in place of the freedom torch. This fantasy could only be depicted graphically, but there is little doubt that, had the manufacturers of St. Jacob's Oil actually been able to replace the French grande dame with a statue of their trademark, they would have jumped at the chance. The abuse of the landscape by a patent medicine mysteriously named S T 1860 brought about the first prohibitive regulation against outdoor advertising in the late 1860s.

Bill posters in the cities during the same period had to

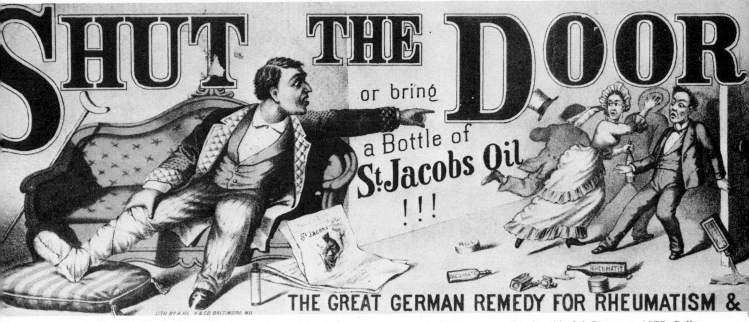

compete for wall space as did their counterparts in Europe before the practice was regulated. In London, it had been a point of honor among billstickers, as the original poster men were called, to paste over the posters of a rival. Before outdoor advertising was regulated in England, billsticking was a dubious profession that required its practitioners to be swift enough to outrun their competitors.

In the United States, the spirit of P. T. Barnum pervaded outdoor advertising after the Civil War. Wagons with posters on their sides traversed the more crowded thoroughfares. Blazing gaslit signs, the forerunners of the huge Times Square electric signs, appeared on buildings, and banners were strung across streets. A favorite ruse of merchants was to hire a man to stand and look intently at one of their posters plastered on a wall. This drew others to stop and read what seemed to be so interesting to him.

The eventual regulation of the hoardings, as the British poster sites were called, brought some order to the display of posters. It prompted the rise of advertising contractors and insured that if an advertiser paid for a display of posters these would remain on view and not be plastered over with someone else's advertisements. Billposting in the United States reached the stage of leased hoardings around the same time as it did in England. One of the first, a fence around the post office site in New York, was leased in 1869. Kissam and Allen, a New York billposting firm, was the first to erect its own boards for posters advertising patent medicines, soaps, perfume, steamships, and other commercial enterprises.

With the growth of the railroads, the train routes became favorite sites for the painting and posting of advertising signs, which were the forerunners of the billboards

In the 1860s and 1870s, it became a game—who could post the last poster. Bill posters, not yet organized into an industry, frequently used the dark of night to place their signs over their competitors'. This drawing shows a London bill station.

designed to be read from moving automobiles.

George Sala, an Englishman who traveled across the United States by train in 1880, protested against

. . . the coarseness and indecency of the quack-salvers' announcements . . . which alarm and disgust the eye at every turn. . . . the loveliest spots in the scenery of this vast continent are blighted with these loathsome stigmata—the portents of shameless imposture and rapacious greed for gold. . . . from New York to San Francisco you are pursued by the quack and his revolting lotions, pills and plasters.

The streetcar card was another means of outdoor advertising. Streetcar advertising, probably inspired by the posters on horse-drawn vans, began about the middle of the nineteenth century when the Lord & Taylor department store started posting advertisements on the New York streetcars. In the 1870s and 1880s, a favorite position for streetcar announcements was near the stove, around which passengers congregated when it got cold. Ads were placed by local merchants until 1884, when Sapolio bought the first streetcar advertising for a national advertiser.

Specialized agencies had been formed to sell streetcar space regionally. Carleton & Kissam, founded in 1889, was the first to sell nationally. To counter the differences in streetcar sizes, they secured widespread adoption of the advertising rack—areas for advertisements—and were instrumental in getting companies to design streetcars in such a fashion that these racks would be prominent. By 1895, Carleton & Kissam controlled the advertising space on nine thousand cars in fifty-four cities, and half a dozen national advertisers were putting between seventy-five thousand and one-hundred thousand dollars a year into streetcar campaigns.

The streetcar cards were posters in miniature. They were wider than they were long, and their design was similar to other forms of outdoor advertising, such as billboards. As streetcars declined, the car cards were used on buses. They were placed inside the buses on racks above the passengers' heads and, in a somewhat larger format, on the sides and backs of the buses.

Lithography firms had begun to dominate the poster business in the 1860s, although woodcut posters were still used well into the 1880s. The lithographic process, invented in 1797 by Alois Senfelder, a German, involved drawing directly on a heavy flat stone with a special crayon that penetrated it. The excess wax was washed away with a mixture of turpentine and water, leaving a printing surface that would accept a greasy ink only where the wax crayon had sunk into the stone. The result was a print that replicated the original crayon drawing. The process made possible a wide range of tones for each color used. Typical early lithographs used only black ink or up to three colors, but, as techniques improved, it was common to find five-color lithographs drawn from as many stones. Eventually, stones were replaced by lightweight zinc plates, which made commercial applications easier.

At first, Americans paid little attention to lithography. This was ironic, since it offered a simple method of approximating the subtle tones of a painting in a way no other reproduction process could rival. It was first used as an art form by Bass Otis, who produced a little black-and-white landscape called "The Mill" in 1819. But its early application in the United States was in commercial fields—the reproduction of sheet music and printing on calico cloth. Gradually, its wider commercial possibilities came to be recognized and a steady stream of popular prints, labels, posters, and trade cards rolled off the presses. By 1848, high-speed printing presses could print ten thousand sheets an hour. This technology made possible the rapid reproduction of large numbers of prints that could be widely distributed. The best-known producers of chromolithographs, or "chromos," for the masses were Nathaniel Currier and J. Merritt Ives, who joined forces in 1850. Their prints, originally in black and white and colored by hand, hung on parlor walls across America. They were purchased by people who could not afford the paintings of the salons but who wanted some form of inexpensive art to hang in their sitting rooms.

Before the widespread use of the halftone, lithography was the quickest means of reproducing pictures and prints of current events. Raging fires, sinking ships, and other newsworthy happenings were quickly drawn by Currier & Ives artists and sold in large editions to the public. Currier & Ives prints were also the primary visual record of American life in the last half of the nineteenth century. Everything was grist for the lithographer's mill, from portraits of presidential candidates to portrayals of whaling expeditions, pictures of clipper ships, and city views.

The popular prints of Currier & Ives influenced the development of the poster tradition in America. They established a vogue for portraying a subject in literal detail and evidenced the most conservative graphic expression. There was no artistic vision in these prints nor any attention given to color or form beyond what was required to tell a story.

The artists who did the original paintings reproduced as lithographs or who drew directly on the stones were mostly Europeans, as were the women who colored each black-and-white print by hand at a wage of less than a penny a print. The artists' lack of experience in America resulted in occasional anomalies, such as a New England wayside inn, painted by an Englishwoman, which was actually a Tudor mansion, and a log cabin, painted by a German, with the door on the gable end.

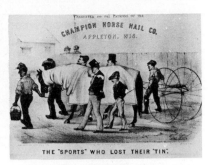

Champion Horse Nail. Poster, c. 1878. Chicago Historical Society. A "before and after" Currier & Ives poster from the 1870s.

Ivory Soap. Billboard, c. 1890. Chicago Historical Society. Courtesy of Procter & Gamble. A later lithographed version of the Ivory soap poster that Harley Procter commissioned from the Strobridge Company in 1883.

Like the artists who created the popular prints, those who established the tradition of chromolithographic advertising posters were first- and second-generation European craftsmen, mostly German and Czech, who preferred the photographlike rendering of a subject to an imaginative interpretation of it. These craftsmen chose to remain anonymous, and there is little information today on who created most of the advertising posters of the nineteenth century. H. C. Bunner, a critic who advocated the poster as a vehicle of artistic expression, referred to the "perverse conservatism" of these anonymous craftsmen who were uninterested in graphic experimentation.

Besides Currier & Ives, other prominent lithographic firms producing posters, prints, and ephemera in the late nineteenth century were Prang & Company, in Boston; Sarony, Knapp & Major, in New York; and the Strobridge Lithographic Company, in Cincinnati. Matt Morgan, an Englishman who joined the Strobridge Company in 1878, was the first artist to sign his posters regularly, although he was essentially a skillful copyist whose illustrative characterizations of actors and actresses could easily have been replaced by photographs.

In the late 1870s, the Strobridge Company exhibited a gigantic poster for the dramatization of *Uncle Tom's Cabin.* The stirring depiction of Eliza's escape across the ice created a sensation. At least one advertiser, Harley Procter of Procter & Gamble, was inspired by it to commission a huge poster from Strobridge in 1883. Procter, who thought in terms of traditional painting rather than bold design, wanted a realistic scene of factory workers washing up with Ivory Soap. To achieve the desired veracity, Strobridge staff artists were posed for a group photograph, which was then superimposed on a painted backdrop depicting a foundry. The composite was then blown up to a twelve-sheet size. Perhaps the largest poster of its day, it was the forerunner of the billboard, which began appearing a few years later.

Occasionally, paintings were adapted for advertising purposes, as was *Westward the Course of Empire*, an heroic mural in the United States Capitol, which, in its poster incarnation, included an industrious farmer driving a McCormick reaper. In England, a vogue developed for using well-known paintings as posters and magazine advertisements. The best example was Sir John Millais's *Bubbles*, a painting of his grandson blowing soap bubbles, which was purchased by the manufacturers of Pear's Soap. There was much debate in England over the use of art for commercial purposes. The more compliant attitude of most of the English art world was probably that expressed by Millais's son, who wrote in his *Life and Letters of Sir John Millais:*

As to Messrs. Pears, I cannot but feel that we ought to be grateful to them for their spirited departure from the beaten track of advertisers. The example they set has tended to raise the character of our illustrated advertisements, whether in pages or posters, and may possibly lead to the final extinction of such atrocious vulgarities as now offend the eye at every turn.

The Frenchman, Jules Chéret, who is acknowledged as the creator of the artistic poster, was the first to exploit the artistic potential of lithography. Before him, lithographers were trained either to transfer paintings or illustrations to stone or else to render naturalistic scenes. Chéret, who learned the technique of chromolithography in England as a young man, made bold drawings directly on stone using as many as five colors. Although the posters he created for Parisian music halls and boulevard theaters, beginning in 1869, brimmed with the gaiety of Parisian night life, he also created some that extolled the virtues of Saxoleine lamps or La Diaphane powder. His large posters were a fixture on the walls of Paris during the *Belle Epoque.* Chéret inspired his fellow artists to try the poster medium. Following his lead were Toulouse-Lautrec, Bonnard, Steinlen, Mucha, and others. The poster activity in Paris also stimulated artists in other European countries, particularly Italy, Belgium, and England.

In England, posters appeared signed by the Beggarstaffs. The Beggarstaffs were actually two artists, James

Pryde and William Nicholson, who usually featured a single image comprised of flat areas of color on a solid colored background. Occasionally, as in their poster for Rowntree's Elect Cocoa, only part of a figure was shown. Their flat color, elimination of detail, and depiction of partial figures were years ahead of the stylistic character of their contemporaries, most of whom still represented a tradition of illustration rather than design.

In the United States in the 1890s, there was a veritable poster renaissance, inspired by the artistic posters being done in Europe. American publishers, in particular, were interested in the European artists and commissioned several—Grasset, Metivet, and Toulouse-Lautrec among them—to create magazine posters. Chéret was never invited; in the American moral climate of the 1890s, Parisian belles kicking up their skirts were considered too risqué. Posters for *Harper's*, *Scribner's*, *Lippincott's*, and other magazines, as well as books and newspapers, were extremely successful and were collected by the public. The popularity of these posters inspired manufacturers to hire some of the young American artists to design advertising posters that were more daring than the conservative lithographs they had been using up to that time. The work of Will Bradley, who was influenced by Beardsley, art nouveau, and the elaborate ornamentation of William Morris, was the most stylized among this group. His posters for Victor Bicycles, Whiting's Standard Papers, and Hood's Sarsaparilla were usually tasteful integrations of type and image, unlike those of most of his contemporaries. Bradley, who had learned the printing trade as a young boy, was one of America's first graphic designers. He could create type, brochures, books, and printer's ornaments as well as posters. His contemporaries—Edward Penfield, Maxfield Parrish, Louis Rhead, Ethel Reed, J. C. Leyendecker and others—were mainly illustrators with less feeling than he had for the integration of typography and image. This was also true of Toulouse-Lautrec, whose magnificent lithographed posters for Aristide Bruant and the *Divan Japonais* usually had poorly drawn letters.

Until the 1890s, posters had been made either from woodcuts or lithographic plates, but the development of halftone printing, initially used for newspapers and magazines, made it possible to reproduce color posters from original art or photography. Process engraving, which approximated the halftone, had been used effectively in the 1880s. Before that, photographs reproduced by lithography were used by the *Canadian Illustrated News* in Montreal in 1869 and later by the New York *Graphic*, an illustrated daily. It was Frederick E. Ives of Philadelphia who invented the halftone process as we know it today. In simple terms, the process broke down a photograph into a series of tiny dots of varying densities; these dots were imposed on a metal plate, which in turn was used to print on paper a close approximation of the original photograph or artwork. By the mid-nineties, it was possible to reproduce color halftones as well as black-and-white ones.

The leaders in the use of art posters for advertising in the 1890s were the bicycle manufacturers. Colonel Albert Pope of Boston had been fascinated with the English highwheeler he saw at the 1876 Centennial Exhibition in Philadelphia. The American version he built had wide appeal to sportsmen. The League of American Wheelmen, formed by highwheeler enthusiasts, had five thousand members by 1881.

It wasn't until the appearance of the safety bicycle in the 1890s, however, that bicycle riding gained widespread popularity. The highwheeler required expert dexterity to maneuver, but anyone could manage a safety bicycle. Models were produced for men and women. Cycling radically altered the American lifestyle. Before the advent of the automobile, the bicycle enabled people to move around the cities and even get out into the country. Cycling also influenced fashions. Women discarded their cumbersome bustles and confining corsets for more comfortable garments that could be worn when cycling.

Apollo Bicycle. Poster, c. 1895. Private collection.

The Pope Manufacturing Company, with its Columbia bicycle, dominated the cycle industry. Along with the Overman Wheel Company, which manufactured the Victor and Victoria cycles, Pope began the extensive advertising that set the bicycle craze in motion. Both firms bought high-quality art for their posters and magazine advertisements. Pope sponsored a poster contest, which was won by Maxfield Parrish; Overman hired Will Bradley to do a series of posters. E. K. Tryon, Jr., & Company commissioned John Sloan to create an artistic poster for their Apollo bicycle. More than any other manufacturers in the 1890s, the bicycle firms improved the quality of advertising art. Their willingness to hire fine artists and tasteful designers gave other manufacturers a new vision of what an advertising poster could be.

While the bicycle craze was at its peak in the mid-nineties, the first automobile appeared. Attempts had been made to operate steam-propelled vehicles on city streets as early as the eighteenth century, but little progress was made until the latter part of the nineteenth century, when many inventors in Europe and America were experimenting with "horseless carriages" driven by steam, electricity, illuminated gas, alcohol, and other substances. In 1886 Gottlieb Daimler in Germany exhibited the first motor tricycle, and the following year his countryman, Carl Benz, produced the first automobile driven by a gasoline engine. It wasn't until 1892 that Charles Duryea and his brother Frank drove the first successful American gasoline car down the streets of Springfield, Massachusetts. By 1895, Duryea was getting competition from Henry Ford, R. E. Olds, and other manufacturers. By the end of the century about eight thousand cars were registered in the United States.

At first, the automobile was promoted as a luxury item and advertising copy stressed the joy of touring along country roads on a Sunday afternoon. The automobile was presented as yet another means of aspiring to a more elegant lifestyle and, as such, became a symbol of upper-class living. The skillful promotion of the automobile as a status symbol was an important factor in the tremendous growth of the industry, and the success of this approach was a strong influence on the promotion of other products as well.

Part of the social change wrought by the automobile was the appearance of the billboard along roads that had formerly served only for the traffic of a few farmers on their way to town. The billboard, placed strategically within view of the drivers who sped past it, became the primary means of outdoor advertising. A well-placed billboard along a roadway could rival in value the boards that lined the major city thoroughfares.

As cities grew and the network of roadways expanded, the production and placement of billboards became an important industry. Eventually, the billboard replaced the poster as the predominant means of outdoor advertising. In 1891, the Associated Bill Posters' Association, a national group of outdoor painting services and poster display firms, was formed. In 1912, the standard twenty-four-sheet size (twelve by twenty-five feet) for billboard posters was adopted, although smaller posters were also used. Standardized billboard sizes meant that manufacturers could place identical advertising on billboards across the country, thus achieving the same breadth of national coverage as could be accomplished with magazines.

Today there are basically three kinds of billboards: boards with printed sheets or panels pasted on them, less usual hand painted signs, and the individual "Spec aculars," which are decorated with inventive forms and neon and flashing lights. The printed posters are the most popular and are generally sold to advertisers for 30-day periods.

Billboard advertising evolved, along with the speed of automobile traffic, to simple pictures and copy. The terse style of writing John Powers initiated in the 1860s came into its own as billboard copy, which had to be read quickly from a moving vehicle. Viewed from distances ranging from 100 to 400 feet, simple messages and large, clear illustrations, in bright and contrasting colors gave billboard advertisements their maximum effect.

Early abuses of the landscape by outdoor advertisers

were attacked by reformers such as Charles Milford Robinson, who wrote in a 1904 issue of *Atlantic Monthly:*

The churches and monuments of Paris have served as boards for despised and fluttering posters; trees have died that their dead trunks might advertise a pill; romantic scenery has been forced to offer reminder of ache or appetite; the glory of the sunset silhouettes against the sky the title of a breakfast food; and the windows of the defenseless home look out on circus girls, corsets, and malt whiskey.

Under pressure from Robinson and other early environmentalists, the outdoor advertising industry drew up a set of guidelines for selecting billboard sites. Nonetheless, the very idea of a billboard on a country road was antithetical to the American tradition of natural landscape, and the billposters remained villains in the eyes of many for years to come.

Duke of Durham Smoking Tobacco. Poster, c. 1870. Collection of Business Americana, Smithsonian Institution. These rather cruel caricatures helped Washington Duke become the largest tobacco merchant of his day.

TOBACCO

Jaw Bone. Mule Ear. Fanny Pan Cake. Lic Quid. It's Naughty But O How Nice. If you think these names are song titles from a rock album, chances are you are not old enough to remember plug chewing tobacco.

Plug was invented in the early nineteenth century to satisfy the cravings of sailors on clipper ships. Not allowed to light their pipes for fear of fires, they started chewing tobacco instead of smoking it. In order to outdo their competitors, farmers and merchants gave their brands whimsical, humorous names, hoping to appeal to the public. The designation was literal; the product was made by drilling holes into trees and plugging them with tobacco leaves. When the tightly packed leaves were cured, the entire tree was cut down and split apart so that the plugs could be easily removed. The hard rectangles of pungent tobacco were then ready to be packaged and sold.

Tobacco as an American industry started in 1613, when the first load of Virginia tobacco arrived in London. Before that time, tobacco was used by the Indians in Mexico as a ceremonial incense and in other parts of the world as a cure for every ailment from the common cold to the plague.

During the sixteenth century, Spanish-grown tobacco was considered the best, but an early Virginia settler, John Rolfe, brought some Spanish seed to the New World, and soon tobacco from the colonies was outselling that grown by the Spanish.

The American Indian, with his pipes of bone, wood, and stone, was responsible for introducing the early colonists to the dubious joys of smoking. The earliest brands of tobacco were shredded and packaged loosely for use in pipes. A French immigrant named Pierre Lorillard, who at age eighteen started his own tobacco company, understood his debt to the American Indian and was responsible for making the statue of an Indian

Sitting Bull Smoking Tobacco. Poster,
c. 1870. Bella C. Landauer Collection,
New York Historical Society. Sitting
Bull ropes a sitting bull. The zinger,
"All other bulls are humbugs," cer-
tainly gets the message across.

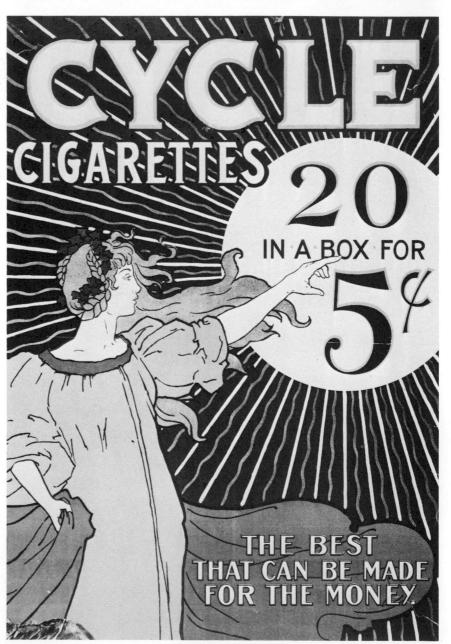

the trademark of tobacconists
the world over.

Early Virginia tobacco became a precious commodity,
as valuable as gold and silver.
It was accepted as payment
for taxes as well as for import-
ing wives from the old country.
During the Revolutionary War,
Gen. George Washington, a tobacco farmer himself, raised
funds for his army with the
slogan: "If you can't send
money, send tobacco."

Just as chewing tobacco
had become popular in the
early nineteenth century, so
did cigar smoking become
fashionable in the latter part
of the same century. "Long
Nines" were thin long cigars of
that time; "Shorts" were somewhat smaller, and "Supers"
were cigars finished off with a
twist. As factories for making
cigars proliferated all over the
country, "Short-Sixes," a combination of several popular
brands, became the standard
most commonly found in tobacco shops and taverns.

Cigarettes were the by-prod-
uct of two wars. During the
1832 war between the Turks
and the Egyptians, soldiers unable to carry their pipes into
battle carried instead a supply
of shredded tobacco and of necessity, they learned to "roll
their own." Cigarettes as we
know them, however, were
born in 1854, during the Cri-
mean War. During one cam-
paign, the English soldiers
captured a train loaded with
Russian troops and their
equipment. Russian-made cigarettes were part of the booty.
The English tried them, found

them superior to what they smoked, and sent the Russian product home to be copied by London tobacconists.

Philip Morris, Esq., was one of the English tobacconists who copied the Russian-made cigarettes. When he perfected his product, he emigrated to America to be close to his source of supply. In 1919, the Philip Morris Company was purchased by Americans and soon became one of the largest tobacco firms in the world. By 1930, one could not enter a drugstore, take a ride in the country, or a walk in the city, without seeing posters and ads, and later hearing the radio voice of Johnny, the smiling Philip Morris midget dressed as a hotel bellman, exclaiming, "Call for Philip Mar-a-iss!"

In the aftermath of the Civil War, Washington Duke started the Duke Tobacco Company, forerunner of the American Tobacco Company, with one barn half-filled with cured tobacco leaves. Thirty years later, Duke was making two hundred cigarettes a minute on his newly invented cigarette-making machine, thus becoming the first mass-producer of cigarettes. Duke's company sold Bull Durham tobacco and Roi-Tan and La Corona cigars, products still on the market today.

JUST A LITTLE.

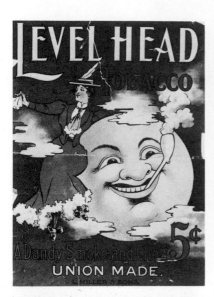

Top: *Level Head Tobacco. Poster, c. 1890. Collection of Business Americana, Smithsonian Institution.* Bottom: *Ball Costumes Cigarettes. Poster, c. 1896. Library of Congress.* The Durham Company believed in the power of the premium and used pictures of "fine ladies of the theatre" to entice smokers to buy their brand and collect the entire series of pictures. The system still works! Another cigarette manufacturer packed paper money into cigarette packages until the U. S. lottery laws caught up with him.

Lorillard's Snuff. Poster, c. 1880. Bella C. Landauer Collection, New York Historical Society.

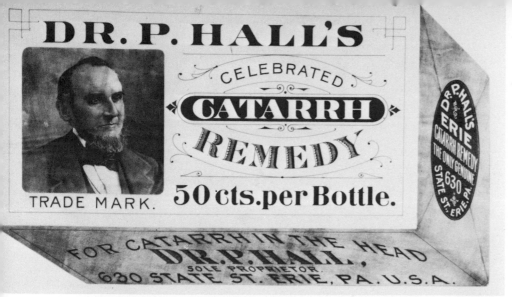

Dr. P. Hall's Catarrh Remedy.
Sign. c. 1890. Collection of Vivian
and Ira Brichta.

Hall's Hair Renewer. Poster, c. 1870. Collection of Business Americana, Smithsonian
Institution.

MEDICAL QUACKERY

Nowhere in the history of advertising were more people deceived than in the area of the fine and ancient art of medical quackery. A strong belief in the folk contention that the seventh son of a seventh son possessed unusual and natural healing powers continued well into the 1880s. Some families called their seventh son "Doctor" while the child was still in diapers. When grown, a seventh son frequently embarked on a self-taught medical career selling home-brewed drugs to a gullible populace.

Wild claims and wild posters went hand in hand during the last quarter of the nineteenth century. The Kennedy Medical Discovery poster, a very early lithograph printed on metal, was used to market that patent medicine shortly after the Civil War. If Kennedy's remedy couldn't cure you of saltrheum or scrofula, a few swigs of the well-advertised Doctor Buckland Scotch Oats Essence or a ride in a Health Jolting chair might.

George Powell's Practical Advertiser, a text on advertising published in 1905, advised its readers that, "the proprietary remedy business is (was) one of the biggest gold mines imaginable." Powell, furthermore, supplied the fundamentals of writing scare copy and instructed untutored medicinemen not to waste a moment, but "to analyze the market and plunge right in."

Lydia E. Pinkham's Vegeta-

Lydia E. Pinkham. Wall sign, c. 1890. Collection of Business Americana, Smithsonian Institution. Mrs. Pinkham did not mention the high alcoholic content of her vegetable compound.

ble Compound made its debut as the "Greatest Medical Discovery Since the Dawn of History" twenty-five years before the turn of the century. Mrs. Pinkham claimed it to be the "ultimate remedy" for female complaints, and by the 1880s, American women were consuming vast quantities of her concoction. Her secret, according to the old posters, was a combination of herbs and salts blended together.

It was Mrs. Pinkham who, in 1891, urged women to "reach for a vegetable instead of a sweet." Forty years later, Lucky Strike cigarettes suggested to women that they "reach for a Lucky instead of a sweet."

Mrs. Pinkham neglected to tell the women of her day, and those still using her medication seventy-five years later, that the "vegetable" compound contained 21 percent alcohol, enough to make most pains seem very far away indeed. Another well-accepted remedy of the Victorian age was Dr. Hostetter's Bitters. Hostetter's medical "discovery" was 44 percent alcohol.

In most cases, the size of the poster could not accommodate a complete list of the diseases and complaints cured by the secret formula advertised. As a result, many of the posters carried the catchall tag line: "... and a lot more for what ails you."

G. A. Shoudy & Sons Soap. Poster, c. 1890. Collection of Business Americana, Smithsonian Institution. France presented the United States with the Statue of Liberty in 1886. Shoudy & Sons used an immigrant maid in the Statue's pose.

50

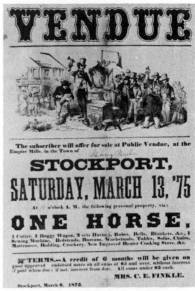

Peerless Washboards. Poster, c. 1890. Collection of Business Americana, Smithsonian Institution. Early stereotype of Chinese as laundry experts. Note the musical jingle fronting the floor:

> *To keep your clothing dry,*
> *A peerless protector buy,*
> *And throw your old washboard up sky high,*
> *your old washboard up sky high.*

Top right: Vendue. Poster, 16" × 20", c. 1875. Collection of Vivian and Ira Brichta. The public auction was an important commercial and social event in small towns in the 1870s. Center right: Baker Horse Blanket. Poster, 11" × 14", c. 1870. Collection of Vivian and Ira Brichta. "Beware of Imitators"; there must have been a lot of horse blanket competition in those days. Bottom right: Grove's Tasteless Chill Tonic. Poster, c. 1880. Collection of Business Americana, Smithsonian Institution. In 1880, blatant or unkind caricatures were perfectly acceptable. Grove's Tonic followed the trend of its era. The claim "No Cure—No Pay" today would translate into a "money back guarantee."

51

PROCTER & GAMBLE

All thy garments smell of myrrh and cassia, out of the ivory palaces, whereby they have made thee glad.

Psalms 45:8.

Harley Procter, son of one of the founders of Procter & Gamble, sat in church one Sunday morning in 1878, preoccupied with a problem. While Harley was kneeling in prayer, his mind was elsewhere, searching for a name for a new product that had been "accidentally" invented by his company.

A batch of white soap had been left alone to churn vigorously in its vat while the worker in charge took an extra-long lunch break. Unwanted air had gotten into the mixture. Afraid to admit his mistake, the soap mixer decided to pack and ship the soap-plus-air combination anyway. The rest is history. All who used the "accidental" soap wanted more, and the Procter & Gamble factory was besieged with new orders. Not only was the product fine, pure, and white, but, mixed with air, it floated.

Sitting in church that Sunday, Harley Procter spotted the word ivory in the book of Psalms: "All thy garments smell of myrrh and cassia, out of the ivory palaces, whereby they have made thee glad."

"That's it," he decided. "I'll call my new white floating soap 'Ivory.'"

That year, P&G spent a few hundred dollars promoting Ivory soap. And, because it

Murphy Varnishes. Poster, c. 1880. Library of Congress. Whimsy, reflective of Alice in Wonderland and Through The Looking Glass, *both published several years earlier.*

52

Big Spring Whiskey. Poster, c. 1890. Library of Congress. A photograph of a nude used as an advertisement was very rare at the turn of the century. This poster must have been carefully tucked into a bar catering only to men.

was a good soap in addition to having a divinely inspired name, Harley's marketing strategy worked.

The early P&G posters documented the fact that there was stiff competition in the soap market. Outstanding among the competitors was the superbly rendered series of posters by the Pears Company. "What the dew is to the flower, Pears Soap is to tender skin," proclaimed one poster, proving that the copywriters of that period were as artistic as were the illustrators. Star soap was promoted as an all-around family product, and the company's posters frequently showed well-scrubbed children at play.

While Procter & Gamble was still a relatively small soap manufacturer in Cincinnati in 1908, the Colgate Company was celebrating its one hundredth year in business and, along with its basic laundry soaps, was already marketing one hundred and sixty kinds of toilet soaps and over two thousand other products.

According to the Colgate Company, P&G was not the first to market a floating soap. In 1864, Caleb Johnson of Milwaukee was selling a soap that floated. Johnson also marketed a body soap he claimed had great cosmetic value since it was made of a mixture of palm and olive oils. He called that soap Palmolive. It was such a success that Johnson named his company, the Palmolive Soap Company.

QUAKER OATS

One of the first cereal products ever to move from the "cracker barrel" into packages was oatmeal. In 1880, Henry Crowell, president of the American Cereal Company, had the prophetic idea that both storekeepers and housewives would prefer to buy oatmeal, America's most popular breakfast food, in boxes of standard size, weight, quality, and price. Henry's real success, however, came after he merged his firm with the Quaker Oats Company and adopted the jovial, rotund, William-Penn-like character as his trademark.

Crowell's early advertising campaigns were extremely ambitious. Broadsides of the Quaker oats man were plastered on buildings across the country, and trains with special "Quaker cars" carried the company's message to every small town in the nation. The Quaker man appeared at state fairs and town celebrations much as Ronald McDonald does today. One overzealous salesman even tried to have the jolly Quaker trademark painted on England's White Cliffs of Dover!

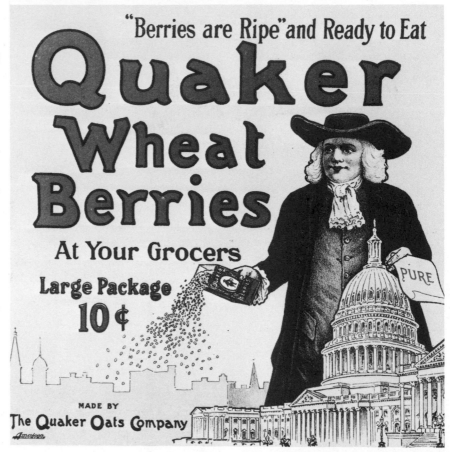

American Extra Dry Champagne. Poster, c. 1870. Library of Congress.

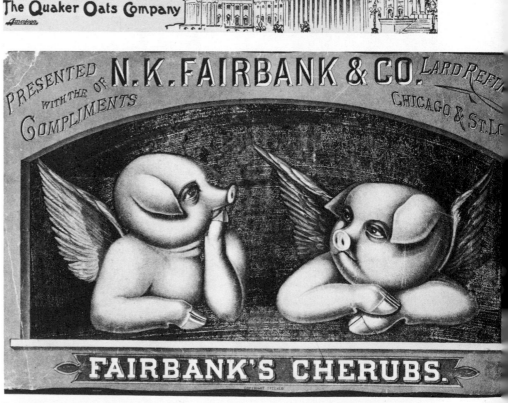

Top: Quaker Wheat Berries. Poster, c. 1910. Collection of Business Americana, Smithsonian Institution. Courtesy of Quaker Oats Company. The William Penn-like character was adopted by Quaker Oats as its trademark in 1877. The Quaker sect represented purity, honesty, strength, and manliness; the company thought this American gentleman fit the bill. Bottom: N. K. Fairbanks Company. Poster, c. 1875. Library of Congress. Humanized winged pigs predated Walt Disney by sixty years. Posters were frequently published as collectors' items and not necessarily to sell services or products.

54

Pettijohn's California Breakfast Food. Poster, c. 1890. Collection of Business Americana, Smithsonian Institution. When Quaker Oats launched its campaign to convert Americans to packaged oats, Pettijohn came along with its slogan: "I eat wheat—my horse eats oats." A pretty girl, a horse, and a country scene; all are elements the artist felt made for high readership. Note how insignificant the cereal box is in the poster.

PLUMBING

"A room with a bath for a dollar and a half." *Statler Hotel, Buffalo, N.Y., 1906.*

The private bath, which includes the luxury of a bathtub, sink, and flush toilet, is a phenomenon of the twentieth century.

Running water, or even the appliances themselves, were not the real hangup. It was the sewage system necessary to carry the water and wastes away without polluting the sources of the water. As soon as municipal sewage systems could match existing water systems, Americans wanted plumbing fixtures. The Statler Hotel in Buffalo, New York, built in 1906, promised "a room with a bath for a dollar and a half." Between 1915 and 1921, the annual production of bathroom and kitchen fixtures for private homes doubled and, by 1925, doubled again, with sales soaring to five million units. Of course, the rich were the first to have water closets. Millard Fillmore had a bath and water closet installed for his use in the White House in 1851, which caused the citizens to call him "unsanitary and undemocratic." Privies were considered more sanitary and a better place to retire to for reasonable privacy.

In 1882, Thomas Crapper, an Englishman, invented the modern flush toilet. The machine-made, mass-produced plumbing fixtures that followed improved the standard of living for millions of Americans during the first quarter of the twentieth century. Among these was the double-shell enameled tub, which became a standard for half a century.

2. Ivory Soap. Poster. c. 1898. Library of Congress. Courtesy of Procter & Gamble.

1. (Preceding page) Kennedy's Medical Discovery. Metal sign. c. 1875. Lithograph on metal, collection of Vivian and Ira Brichta. Kennedy promised relief for every ailment known to man. The company did a thriving business: its product contained 40 percent alcohol! The allegorical character is using his heavenly powers to slay dreaded diseases.

3

4

3. Kingsford's Starch. Poster, c. 1900.
Library of Congress. Women alone with
their thoughts: a forerunner of Edward
Hopper's paintings.
4. Bell's Soapona Soap. Poster, c. 1889.
Library of Congress.

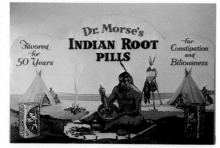

5. Duluth Imperial Flour. Poster, c. 1890. Library of Congress. A ride in a balloon was part of turn-of-the-century country fair fun. The aerial view is unusual for the posters of that era.
6. Dr. Morse's Indian Root Pills. Window sign, 50″ × 20″, c. 1890. Collection of Vivian and Ira Brichta. The story goes . . . Dr. Morse was trading with the Indians when word arrived that Grandfather was close to death. Dr. Morse rushed home with a medicine man and his famous Root Pills. After treatment Grandfather recovered, and Dr. Morse returned to the wilds.
7. Frank Miller's Crown Dressing. Poster, 12″ × 20″, c. 1880. Collection of Vivian and Ira Brichta. The artistic lettering is in keeping with the elegance of the setting and the figure.

8. Strouse & Brothers. Poster, c. 1888. Library of Congress. Fashionable cloth ing was featured by this retail store.

9. Hodgman's Mackintoshes. Poster, c. 1881. Library of Congress. Superb street scene complete with electric lights, horsedrawn carriage, and, of course, the latest in rainwear. The poster is executed in the manner of *The Place de l'Europe on a Rainy Day,* a painting by French artist Gustave Caillebotte.

11

12

11. New York Enamel Paint Company.
Poster, c. 1890. Library of Congress.
This genre scene may mean that the
manufacturer wanted to sell his paint to
the wealthy.

12. Café Du Monde Coffee. Poster, c.
1890. Library of Congress.

. Wheeler & Wilson No. 9. Poster, c.
'0. Library of Congress. This expen-
machine was for the "elite" trade
se taste was reflected in the quality
nishings.

13

15

14

13, 14. Bock Beer. Posters, c. 1870–1880. Library of Congress.
15. Frank Fehr Bock Beer. Poster, 28″ × 40″, c. 1880. Collection of Vivian and Ira Brichta.

16

16. Black and Tan. Poster. c. 1898. Library of Congress.
17. American Brewing Company. Poster. c. 1896. Library of Congress.
18. Joseph Schlitz. Poster. c. 1890. Library of Congress. Courtesy of Joseph Schlitz Brewing Company. Schlitz used this unauthorized testimonial by President Grover Cleveland.

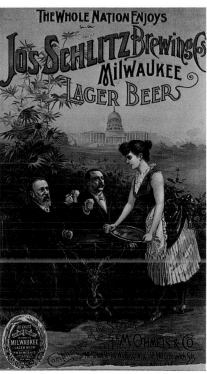

18

17

The FRIENDLY ROAD

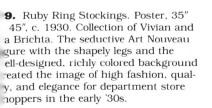

21. YWCA. Poster, c. 1930. Collection of Vivian and Ira Brichta.

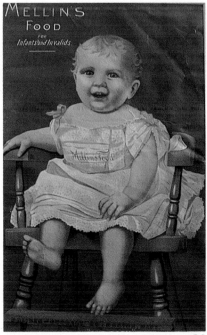

MELLIN'S FOOD *For Infants and Invalids*

20. Anheuser-Busch. Poster, c. 1885. Library of Congress. Adolphus Busch, a corporal in the Missouri National Guard during the Civil War, married the daughter of Eberhard Anheuser and joined the 10-year-old Anheuser Brewery as a salesman. The brewery developed pasteurization and was able to ship beer over long distances. In 1878, the company won an international award for excellence in Paris, a first for an American brewer.

22. Kellogg's Corn Flakes. Poster, 60″ × 40″, c. 1895. Collection of Vivian and Ira Brichta. Reprinted with permission of Kellogg Company. Kellogg's had to convince Americans, brought up on cooked, hot oatmeal breakfasts, to switch to cold packaged cereals. The fresh, crispy taste of corn flakes and its convenience for the housewife turned oatmeal lovers into cold cereal enthusiasts.

23. Mellin's Foods. Poster, 22″ × 26″ c. 1895. Collection of Vivian and Ira Brichta. "Our Baby," painted in a traditional early American naive style with appropriate hand lettering.

9. Ruby Ring Stockings. Poster, 35″ 45″, c. 1930. Collection of Vivian and a Brichta. The seductive Art Nouveau gure with the shapely legs and the ell-designed, richly colored background reated the image of high fashion, qual-y, and elegance for department store hoppers in the early '30s.

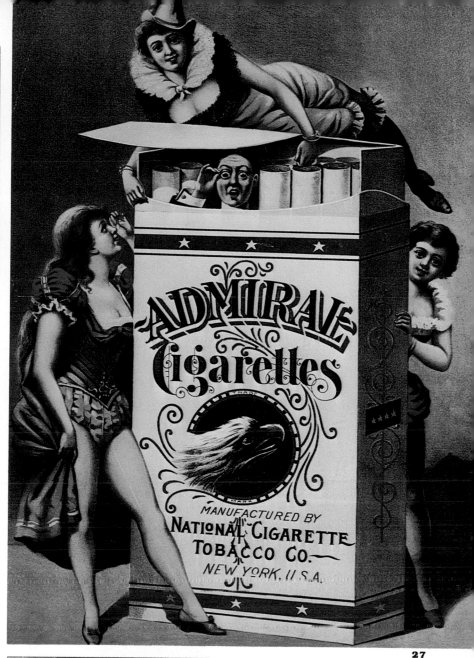

25. C. Vowinkel & Company. Poster, c. 1880. Library of Congress. Wine selling with a Frans Hals touch. Poster artists frequently looked to the fine arts for inspiration.

26. New Early Sunrise Potato. Poster, 10″ × 15″, c. 1880. Collection of Vivian and Ira Brichta. The humanized potato proved a charming way to catch the public's eye.

Arrow Collars and Shirts. Sign, c. 7. Library of Congress. Courtesy of w Shirt Company, a division of t, Peabody and Company. Illustra- by J. C. Leyendecker.

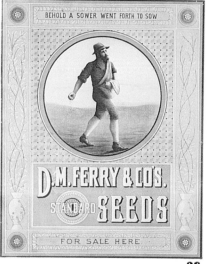

27. Admiral Cigarettes. Poster, c. 1890. Library of Congress. Enlarged package and fantasy characters tie cigarettes into having a good time.

28. D. M. Ferry Seeds. Poster, 24″ × 30″, c. 1880. Collection of Vivian and Ira Brichta. Ferry Seeds used that subtle-sell approach to project a conservative image of quality and reliability.

29. Samuel Woodside Company. Poster. c. 1870. Library of Congress. The name "Laugh At" Cigars appears five times in this poster—but you've got to look for it!

30. Richmond Straight Cut and Virginia Brights. Poster. c. 1890. Library of Congress.

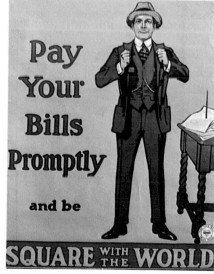

31. The Flying Merkel. Poster. c. 1915. Library of Congress.
32. YMCA. Poster. c. 1920. Collection of Vivian and Ira Brichta.

31

32

33. (Overleaf) Between the Acts Cigarettes. Poster. c. 1890. Library of Congress. Little Nell, heroine of "The Drunkard," one of the most popular saloon plays of the decade, showed up in posters as well as on stage. Between The Acts Cigarettes is one of the few surviving tobacco brands, even though the name was switched from cigarettes to cigars sometime between 1890 and 1930.

COCA-COLA

Coca-Cola was first introduced as a fountain syrup in the 1890s, and the name, the symbol, and the color quickly became an integral part of the American scene. The outdoor billboards, the posters, and the advertisements on back covers of the Saturday Evening Post all helped make Coca-Cola the best-known soft drink in the world—perhaps the best-known brand of anything in the world!

Even in its earliest days, the Coca-Cola Company believed that establishing a good brand name and continually enhancing that name were critical to the success of their product. Consequently, Coke ads have appeared on truck panels, walls of buildings, lamp shades, clock faces, pencil boxes, and serving trays; Coca-Cola was, and continues to be, almost everywhere one looks.

Coke posters have always been carefully designed to display bright, attractive, desirable images reflective of the best of every era. Beautiful people in ads and posters have, in effect, said "Coke and I are the best of 1909 or 1916 or 1926." Today, Coca-Cola art still follows that same wholesome tradition.

The bright red metal open-top Coke cooler became a fixture in virtually every American drugstore in the late twenties. At about the same time, Coke introduced its famous six-pack; it was convenient for the consumer and an excellent way to sell six bottles of Coke instead of one. No wonder the then newly popular chain stores and the self-service food markets loved the innovative merchandising of the Coca-Cola Company.

During the radio days of the forties, Coke posters, promotions and six-packs became familiar ambassadors of decoration and refreshment to people all over the world.

Coke and Coca-Cola are registered trademarks of the Coca-Cola Company.

Top: Coca-Cola. Poster, c. 1918. Courtesy of Coca-Cola Company. Coca-Cola is a registered trademark of the Coca-Cola Company. Bottom; Coca-Cola Company. Poster, c. 1890. Collection of Business Americana, Smithsonian Institution. Coca-Cola is a registered trademark of the Coca-Cola Company.

things go
better
with
Coke

Coca-Cola. Poster, c. 1964. Courtesy of Coca-Cola Company. Coca-Cola is a registered trademark of the Coca-Cola Company.

Kodak. Poster, c. 1896. Private collection. Kodak used an illustration rather than a photograph to boost a travel-oriented lifestyle.

KODAK

George Eastman, in the classic tradition of Horatio Alger, started his career as a floor sweeper, cuspidor cleaner, and messenger boy in Rochester, New York. With genius and determination, he started a dozen industries and helped create several new branches of science and medicine and one basic art form.

In 1880, Eastman perfected a process for manufacturing dry plates for newspaper photographs that made it easier to include pictures in daily editions. He then developed a sensitive film that could be used for indoor and outdoor photography.

Eastman introduced the Kodak camera in 1888. It was a small, lightweight, box camera, completely different from the large, pack-horse type of equipment used in those days. The Kodak came from the factory loaded with enough film to make one hundred prints and it sold for twenty-five dollars. "You press the button, we do the rest" was the slogan that brought the Kodak camera to the world through magazine and poster advertisements.

For a decade after its birth, each Kodak camera, complete with exposed film, had to be returned to Rochester for developing and reloading. In 1891, the Eastman Company found a way to put transparent film on a spool so that it could be loaded by the individual owner. By simplifying the camera and the film, Eastman created a world of leisure-time photographers. According to Eastman, "Anyone who could push a button could take pictures."

George Eastman's contribution to photography has been compared with Gutenberg's invention of movable type as instruments of the most facile means of spreading knowledge. The development of the camera created breakthroughs in medical research, astronomy, science, and industry, as well as in entertainment and advertising. The familiar red-and-yellow film box has become a traveling companion for millions and it gave rise to hundreds of businesses that sell and process film.

From the very inception of the Kodak camera, the company believed in advertising. Two years before the twentieth century began, the Eastman Company invested over seven hundred and fifty thousand dollars in advertising, a record expenditure.

Even though kodak (in its early days a lower case k was used) sold photography, an 1895 poster featured an artist's drawing of a woman with her box camera photographing a foreign shore. A Kodak executive commented at the time, "We used photographs in our posters until our competition started doing the same thing; we also discontinued the photos because they did not give a fair idea of the quality of the work a camera could do." In those days, the photoengraving process had not been perfected and photographs were not good enough for use in ads, especially by camera manufacturers.

As advertising developed, more and more advertisers turned from poster artists to photographers to present their products with realism and drama. The greatest leap in that direction took place immediately after World War I. By the middle of the 1950s, professional advertising source books listed four to eight times the number of commercial photographers as commercial illustrators.

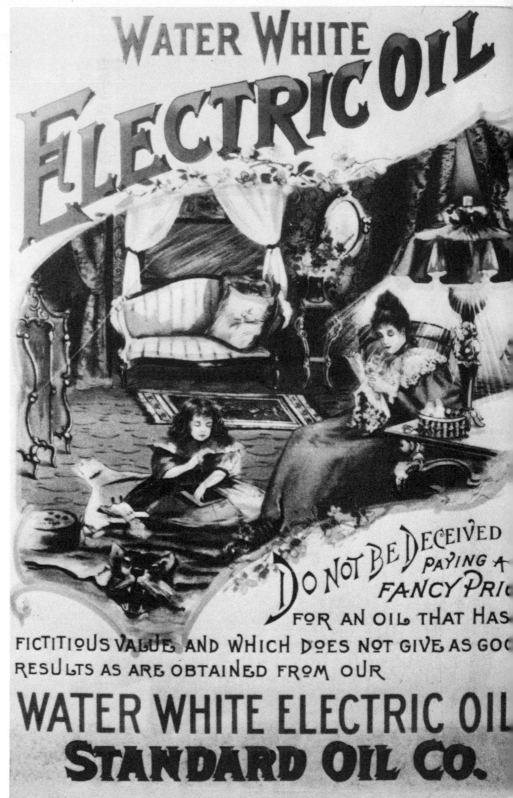

Water White Electric Oil. Poster, 12" × 15", c. 1880. Collection of Vivian and Ira Brichta. The label says "The Standard Oil Company" but it has not been substantiated that this pre-Victorian oil lamp was made by the present-day Standard Oil Company.

60

CHAPTER THREE
BULLETS, BEGGARS, AND BATHTUB GIN: 1900-1945

During the second half of the nineteenth century, the American standard of living had improved considerably, although, in 1900, the gulf between the rich and the emerging middle class was still enormous. At the turn of the century, farmers and villagers were flocking to the large urban centers, where they could earn enough money to enjoy the comforts and conveniences that were quickly defining the new middle-class lifestyle.

Outdoor signs in San Francisco, c. 1920. Foster & Kleiser.

Few people expected to attain the wealth of a Carnegie or a Morgan. Most aspired to a comfortable middle-class life, an ideal that attracted vast numbers of foreign immigrants to American cities in the late nineteenth and early twentieth centuries. The immigrants were ambitious, yet unfamiliar with the American language and customs. They quickly filled the ranks of the factory workers and took jobs that didn't require much understanding of American commerce. In spite of poor working conditions and low wages, they gradually improved their lot and their places were filled by newer immigrants.

The economic betterment of the immigrant class at the beginning of the century was indicative of a general improvement in finances. Businesses were growing from "mom and pop" stores to multimillion-dollar enterprises. This phenomenal expansion was aided by the growing appreciation of the role of advertising in creating mass sales.

Advertising was a shortcut to the improvement of sales

that had taken many years to accomplish by person-to-person selling. Phillip D. Armour, the Chicago meat-packer once asked D. M. Lord, the well-known advertising executive, why his company should spend money on advertising when his products were so well distributed throughout the country. Lord replied that distribution systems didn't reach consumers and that advertising encouraged them to ask for specific advertised brands. Armour was convinced, and from that time on Armour & Company was an advertiser.

Part of advertising's success was due to the growing sophistication of its methods and practices. There was an increasing recognition of the value of continuity, maintaining a set of characteristics through a series of advertisements so that each new one related to those that preceded it. This meant presenting one new idea per advertisement until all the arguments for the product had been exhausted, and then starting all over again. In 1902 this was called "serial advertising," an approach that eventually evolved into the themes and variations that are now part of most campaigns.

Today, Raleigh and Winston cigarettes, Kraft Foods, and other major outdoor advertisers strive in their billboard series for a visual continuity that corresponds to continuity in copy.

In March 1901, *Publicity*, an advertising periodical, prophesied:

The time is not far away when the advertising writer will find out the inestimable benefits of a knowledge of psychology. . . . An advertisement has been written to describe the article which it has wished to place before the reader; a bit of cleverness, an attractive cut, or some other catchy device has been used, with the hope that the hit or miss ratio could be made as favorable as possible. But the future must be full of better methods than these to make advertising advance with the same rapidity as during the latter part of the last century.

Occasional articles on the psychology of advertising had appeared in advertising publications as early as 1895, but none had the far-reaching effect of Walter Dill Scott's series, "The Psychology of Advertising," which was published in the *Atlantic Monthly* in 1903. Scott, then a professor of psychology at Northwestern University, pointed out the defects of current advertising copy. He emphasized the need for cheerful advertisements. According to him, patent medicine manufacturers who showed victims of one ailment or another in pain were on the wrong track. He criticized advertizers who linked their products, even as a joke, with bulls, pigs, frogs, and other less than engaging creatures. This was an approach used often in nineteenth-century posters; winged pigs, stubborn bulls, and even Palmer Cox's little brownies were associated with lard, tobacco, and rubber boots.

Scott shifted the focus of advertising from explaining

how an article worked to describing the pleasure it could give the user. "How many (advertisers) describe an undergarment so that the reader can feel the pleasant contact with his body?" he questioned. "Many advertisers seem never to have thought of this, and make no attempt at such description." Heeding Scott's advice, the advertising profession began to adopt the terminology of the psychologist.

Advertising agencies had begun to shift in the 1890s from primarily selling space to handling other phases of a client's campaign. This transition occurred by degrees over a period of about twenty years. It was a result of necessity; manufacturers were spending more on their advertising and demanding better service from their agencies. The agencies, in turn, sought the best talent available. Successful newspaper writers were among those hired to write advertising copy. Prospective agency writers were also hired away from advertising staffs of newspapers; employees of printing houses who were familiar with the special typographic requirements of advertisements formed another group from which to draw.

The agencies began to give greater importance to illustration, which until 1900 had done little more than draw attention to the product. Agency art departments were formed. Before 1900 a freelance artist would be called in and given instructions on how to depict the product, but after that time illustrations were planned with the close cooperation of the agency's own artists. Many of the agency staff artists had previously worked for newspapers, covering news events with the reporters as photographers do today. Having inhouse agency artists resulted in a greater use of pictorial copy to sell the product by showing it in use or in an atmosphere that made it look desirable.

Another function that the advertising agency assumed was research. Around 1910 departments were started in many agencies to gather market data nationwide. Advertising plans based on these data resulted in copy derived from detailed knowledge of the product, its market, and its uses rather than from the clever ideas of "literary men." The whimsey and hyperbole of earlier decades were replaced by simple slogans.

The man who pioneered the techniques of researching consumer wants and buying habits was Charles Coolidge Parlin. He was a young schoolteacher hired by the *Saturday Evening Post* to determine the wants and habits of its readers in order to improve the magazine's sale of advertising space. Parlin called his work "commercial research." Eventually he moved on to a study of markets for almost every product in America's hundred largest cities. His information was based on the study of the volume of sales and kinds of merchandise stocked in every department, dry-goods, and men's ready-to-wear store in each of these cities. Parlin's techniques evolved into the sophisticated method of market research, which enabled manufacturers to test the demand for a new product before they ever produced it.

At the beginning of the twentieth century the techniques of the advertising profession were ahead of its ethics. There was widespread public outrage against false or extravagant claims, evidenced particularly in patent medicine advertising. This response was part of a larger questioning of American business practices that, at its best, sprang from a deep idealism and concern for fairness and equality; at its worst, it was a kind of muckraking intended primarily to sell newspapers and magazines. The advertising of reputable manufacturers did not make exaggerated claims. The patent medicine manufacturers, however, had been hoodwinking the public for decades and bore the brunt of the public's attack. The result was the passage of the Food and Drug Act of 1906, which forced the patent medicine manufacturers to tone down their claims and list the ingredients of their nostrums. The Food and Drug Act was a sign that America was growing up, that consumers would no longer allow manufacturers to take their hard-earned money in exchange for false promises or shoddy goods.

After 1900, a national distribution system began to fall into place. Larger and more powerful locomotives hauled an ever-increasing volume of freight along the vast network of railroad lines that by then linked the nation from coast to coast. Chain stores continued to spread. With their bulk orders, these stores could cut prices and entice more consumers. The Piggly Wiggly, a self-service grocery chain, was a leading rival of the A&P. The first Piggly Wiggly opened in 1916. Its distinctive feature was a maze of aisles through which customers had to pass to reach the exit. There were no salespersons to recommend particular brands; customers were on their own and had to make their selections based on previous knowledge of the products derived from newspapers, magazines, posters, or billboards. The package became more important as a selling tool since brands competed with each other and customers frequently chose a product because of the appeal of the package rather than its contents.

Package design became a separate profession. The research methods that the advertising agencies were employing for the preparation of copy stimulated package designers to investigate the effect of a package's color, shape, and size on the customer's purchasing choices. The psychological approach to advertising that Walter Dill Scott had articulated led to elaborate experiments in this area.

Self-service food stores caught on quickly. In California,

Top: By 1930, the Sunkist brand was so well known that designers could take liberties with it—in this case by partially obliterating it. Institute of Outdoor Advertising. Sunkist is a trademark of the Sunkist Growers, Inc. Reprinted with permission of Sunkist Growers, Inc. Bottom: Great density of traffic, pedestrians, and buildings—the perfect backdrop for dozens of billboards during the 1920s. Institute of Outdoor Advertising.

Heinz Baked Beans. Billboard, c. 1930. Metropolitan Museum of Art. Henry J. Heinz started by selling home-made horseradish to his neighbors. He became one of the marketing geniuses of his time, producing hundreds of food products rather than the "57" that symbolizes his firm.

Campfire Marshmallows. Tin package, c. 1920. Collection of Vivian and Ira Brichta.

in the 1920s, the drive-in market was a popular response to the automobile. Another new shopping institution was the supermarket, an idea that became widespread in the 1930s. The supermarket combined self-service with wide variety; groceries, meats, vegetables, and dairy products were all available under one roof. Improvements in refrigeration equipment enabled the supermarkets to bring foods from around the country and to prolong their shelf-life. Shoppers went to the store less often but purchased larger quantities of food for home storage. In 1921, only five thousand household refrigerators were sold in the United States; a decade later, sales were in excess of one million, and by 1950, over 90 percent of American homes had refrigerators.

Refrigeration radically altered the American diet. Even though refrigerated railroad cars had been used to ship meat by rail as early as 1881, fruit and vegetable growers were slow to use this mode of transport. People had to rely on locally grown produce and were without fresh fruits and vegetables during the winter and early spring, when they consumed large quantites of bread, pies, potatoes, and other starchy foods.

The automobile brought about the most drastic changes in twentieth-century life. Henry Ford introduced his famous Model T in 1908. "Let them have any color they want," he said at a meeting in 1914, "so long as it's black." During the first quarter of the twentieth century, over fifteen million black Model T's known as "Tin Lizzies" were sold—some for as little as two hundred and ninety dollars. Other manufacturers tried to compete with Ford by designing new body styles and christening their vehicles with appealing names like Jackrabbit, Bearcat, Bulldog, and Playboy. Few could compete with Ford's assembly-line regularity, but General Motors' Alfred Sloan, who took that company's reins in 1923, began to give Ford a run for his money. Sloan built up the Chevrolet, which he called a "mass-class" car

Libby's Meats. Calendar poster, 28" × 35", c. 1893. Collection of Vivian and Ira Brichta. In 1882, Libby, McNeill & Libby developed a tapered tin can in which beef could be packed and preserved, and Libby became not only the largest packer of corned beef, but a prominent packer of fruits, vegetables, juices, and frozen products as well.

Baker Electric. Handbill, 10" × 14", c. 1895. Collection of Vivian and Ira Brichta.

AUTOMOBILES

The names of automobiles from the past are enough to make any car enthusiast grab his goggles, duster, and girl friend and race into a setting sun. Garland, Owen, Winston, Kissel were only a few of the hundreds of cars made over the years. There was the Darling, Maxwell, Essex, Reo, and the Haynes, and, of course, the Pierce Arrow and Overland. Unfortunately, the best of American engineering and marketing skills was not enough to save these companies as they merged into larger firms or went out of business.

Top: Fisk Tires. Billboard, c. 1929. Private collection. Bottom: Jewett Auto. Billboard, c. 1922. Private collection.

as opposed to Ford's mere "mass" car. Sloan recognized the public's taste for newer and larger automobiles, and his car had "a bigger package of accessories and improvements beyond basic transportation."

Sloan's flashier Chevrolet made the Model T look like an antique. Ford shut down his plant in early 1927 and geared up to produce a new car to compete with General Motors. When the Model A was announced later in the year, the public was so anxious to see it that lines formed in front of showrooms twenty-four hours before the first cars were delivered. The public could have its choice of Niagara Blue, Versailles Violet, Arabian Sand, and other colors. An automobile trade magazine reported that over one-quarter of the American population saw the Model A during its first week off the assembly lines. "He's Made a Lady Out of Lizzie" became a popular song of the day.

But Ford faced stiff competition. The disc-wheeled Chevrolet was moving in on the market with great speed; so was the new Dodge. The Jewett, Reo, Buick, Willys, Stern Knight, Overland, and Pontiac were also competing for the growing market in the late twenties, and the air-cooled Franklin, along with Pierce-Arrow, Packard, Kissel, Jordan, Auburn Dusenberg, Marmon, and Templar were challenging the Cadillac, Lincoln, and Chrysler in the higher-priced market.

At first, automobile advertising illustrations depicted unoccupied cars and were similar in style to the drawings found in mail-order catalogs. Soon advertisements showed cars being driven. Early automobile copy stressed the joys of touring as well as the mechanical perfection of the vehicles themselves. Cars such as the Overland were often pictured with the driver in the front seat and his family behind, the whole set against a rural background. The presentation of the open touring car as a leisure-time vehicle prepared the way for the upper-class appeal in advertising copy. The automobile was pictured as a luxury for the rich, particularly after the advent of the closed car. Pierce-Arrow advertisements around 1915—with illustrations by Edward Penfield, J. C. Leyendecker, and other well-known illustrators— showed elegant couples leaving fancy establishments and stepping off curbs into vehicles driven by expressionless chauffeurs. Around the same time, a heavy volume of automobile accessory advertising helped build interest and confidence in the automobile. Tire advertising, particularly by Fisk and Goodyear, became widespread, as did the promotion of spark plugs, batteries, and other parts.

The words that President Calvin Coolidge delivered to the International Advertising Association's Washington convention in 1926 are applicable to the automobile's development as a form of transportation accessible to the masses:

The preeminence of American industry, which has constantly brought about a reduction of costs, has come very largely through mass production. Mass production is only possible where there is mass demand. Mass demand has been created almost entirely through the development of advertising.

Mass production also enabled America to gear up for World War I. President Wilson pointed out the magnitude of the conflict in a speech on May 18, 1917: "In the sense in which we have been wont to think of armies there are no armies in this struggle, there are entire nations armed. . . . The whole Nation must be a team in which each man shall play the part for which he is best fitted." The burgeoning advertising industry, which had already become part of the fabric of American life, was called upon to help promote the nationwide war effort. Representatives of the advertising community formed themselves into a group to assist the Council of National Defense. The group soon became the Division of Advertising of the Committee of Public Information. Headed by George Creel, editor of the *Rocky Mountain News*, it was known by most people as the Creel Committee. Government officials, particularly army brass, were suspicious of advertising. They preferred orders and edicts to techniques of mass persuasion. Nonetheless, the advertising men persisted and soon proved advertising's efficacy. Posters, magazines, and newspapers announced the wheatless, meatless days dreamed up by Herbert Hoover's Food Administration to save food. Patriotic themes abounded: George Washington, Thomas Jefferson, and other American heroes called upon the public to support Red Cross drives, sell conservation, and buy Liberty bonds. Posters and billboards were used extensively for recruiting and for many other purposes in support of the war effort.

Manufacturers took what opportunities they could to link their product sales to the war effort or at least to keep their brand names before the public. Kodak took full-page magazine ads to encourage families to cheer up the boys overseas by sending them snapshots from home or, better yet, sending them cameras so they could take their own snapshots. Everyone was "Stepping on to Victory" on Cat's Paw Rubber Heels, and uniformed doughboys proclaimed that "Aunt Jemima Rings the Bell with Me."

Following the post-World War I recession in the early twenties, the national income took a quantum leap. Manufacturing facilities, greatly expanded during the war, were available for producing goods in a volume far exceeding prewar needs. The 1920s was a period of extremes. Those who had little before the war now wanted all the luxuries of the rich. Selling became as important as production, and aggressive salesmen were the new heroes of commerce.

The day of the order-taker was over. Management directed sales staffs to go out and find customers rather

Top: Goggles. Store sign, c. 1920. Private collection. Glasses could enhance the feeling of flying down the open road. Bottom: Fisk Tires. Billboard, c. 1918. Private collection. Illustration by Maxfield Parrish.

Bromo-Seltzer. Billboard, c. 1917. Collection of Business Americana, Smithsonian Institution. Courtesy of Warner-Lambert Company.

than wait for the orders to come to them. Selling as a profession began to attract more aggressive individuals who were interested in such incentives as sizable commissions, sales contests, and a chance to advance in the company. Success was measured by an ability to maintain a positive mien and a steady flow of orders.

The salesman was joined in the labor force by an increasing number of women. Before World War I, only about 20 percent of American women worked for a living. Business was still a man's profession, and the offices, clubs, and restaurants where business was conducted were considered male preserves. Most women still believed that their place was in the home. Some professions were associated with easy virtue. A nicely brought up woman might become a teacher or a nurse but an actress was known as a "fast" woman. Such attitudes changed somewhat in the course of World War I, when large numbers of women were called into the labor force to replace the men at the front. During this time they made measurable gains in industry assisted by a sympathetic government. President Wilson called for equal wages for men and women doing the same work—a bold idea at the time. Although this was not always carried out in practice, it was at least publicly promoted and led to eventual means of combating wage discrimination. Women were also appointed to key industrial boards, and leading defense organizations had their women's committees. When the war ended, many women, who were enjoying the new freedom and independence, remained in the labor force. They became a new consumer class, a fact that manufacturers were quick to recognize. Soon a plethora of products was being manufactured especially for women.

Women's fashions quickly changed to reflect this new status. During the war, women working as stetcher-bearers, ambulance drivers, and factory hands—occupations previously filled by men—discovered that it was more convenient to wear their hair short. They had little time for elaborate coiffures and there were also health hazards to long hair— women in ammunition factories found that gunpowder got into it. The newspapers carried photographs of working women with bobbed hair wearing overalls and knickers, and other women who became aware of the comfort and timesaving qualities of short hair were soon invading one of the last bastions of male exclusivity, the barbershop. One barber in California, aiming to satisfy his long-time customers, put out a sign, "Barbershop for Men Only."

By 1924, bobbed hair had become almost universal. It showed signs of dying out at the end of the war, but was revived by movie actresses such as Clara Bow. Nearly all the spring hats of 1924 were so small they would fit only women with bobbed hair. Concomitantly, corsets were thrown off, skirts were shortened by half, and silk or rayon lingerie replaced heavier undergarments. Brassieres were designed to flatten the breasts. Flesh-colored silk stockings took the place of unappealing cotton and became one of the most important fashion innovations of the twentieth century. Younger women were the first to take up these new styles; older women followed more slowly and, in some cases, reluctantly.

The slim, flat-chested woman epitomized the new look of the twenties. In the motion picture theaters, Clara Bow, the "It" girl, puckered her lips, pressed her knees together, and excited the young men of the Jazz Age.

Not everyone embraced the new styles with enthusiasm. There were many comments on what San Francisco journalist Wallace Irwin called the "increased decrease" of women's clothing. "Give feminine fashions time enough and they will starve all the moths to death," wrote a prudish journalist in the Detroit *Free Press* in June 1925. A widely quoted joke of the day referred to the old sailor who remarked that he supposed the girls wore their dresses at half-mast as a mark of respect to departed modesty. In a more serious vein, George W. Neville, president of the New York Cotton Exchange, deplored the scantiness of women's undergarments, which "has reduced consumption of cotton fabrics by at least twelve yards of finished goods for each adult female inhabitant."

The cosmetics industry, soon to top one billion dollars in annual sales, blossomed. The vogue for rouge and lipstick—once considered signs of a loose woman—spread swiftly. Beauty shops sprang up everywhere to give facials, set hair, and otherwise make women feel more youthful and appealing. By 1929, a pound of face powder for every woman in the country was being sold annually. At that time, no less than twenty-five hundred brands of perfume and fifteen hundred face creams were on the market.

The rejection of stodgy codes of dress and the use of cosmetics were matched by a radical change in social customs, particularly a sharp increase in smoking and drinking by women. The flapper, whom F. Scott Fitzgerald and John Held, Jr., made famous, was as much at home in a speakeasy as she had previously been in her parents' parlor.

Women and men socialized in public more frequently. Mixed drinking led to a new social institution, the cocktail party. People crowded into the new nightclubs, which varied from a hole in the wall to elaborate rooms with restaurants and jazz bands. During prohibition these were well-guarded and often mixed up with gangland activities.

Politically, the liberation of women was signified by the passage, in 1920, of the Nineteenth Amendment, which

Atlantic Gasoline. Billboards. c. 1926. Private collection. In 1920, the 19th Amendment gave women the vote. On the way to the voting booths, America's women moved into the labor force, learned to drive the family car, and smoked in public.

69

gave women the right to vote. The entrance of women into the labor force and into the political system were major steps on the long road to corporate executive positions and top political offices.

Paradoxically, the looser moral attitudes of the twenties went hand in hand with one of the most repressive pieces of legislation ever passed by the United States Congress. The Eighteenth Amendment, which went into effect in January 1920, prohibited the manufacture, transportation, or sale of intoxicating beverages. Even worse than the Eighteenth Amendment was the Volstead Act, passed immediately afterward, which legislated its enforcement. The Volstead Act defined an alcohlic beverage as one containing one-half of 1 percent alcohol, which ruled out most drinks including beer, wine, and of course whiskey.

The amendment slipped through congress, which had little conception of the problems it would create. One reason for its passage was that the temperance groups and other forces who favored it were tightly organized while those who opposed it—notably the liquor industry, which at the time had a somewhat unsavory reputation—were not. Another factor that helped passage of the Volstead Act was the wartime call for sacrifice and sobriety. The war had also turned the public against everything German, including some of the nation's largest brewers and distillers.

Prohibition was impossible to enforce. In 1920, there were only 1,520 agents to police the whole country. This number had grown by 1930 to a mere 2,836, a force hardly sufficient to police the extensive borders, speakeasies, illicit stills, industrial alcohol manufacturers, and druggists who were licensed to sell alcohol on doctor's prescriptions. Liquor was smuggled into the country by every possible means— rum ships from Bimini, freighters with contraband gin mixed among legitimate cargo, and freight cars full of whiskey smuggled across the Canadian border.

Alcohol was consumed in hip flasks at football games, at speakeasies, in hotel rooms, at conventions, and was delivered to homes by young men sent from nearby "service stations."

The Eighteenth Amendment failed to curb the national intake of alcoholic beverages and, by making their manufacture and distribution illicit, spawned the Al Capones, Dean O'Bannions, and other bootleggers who battled each other with sawed-off shotguns throughout the twenties. When, on December 5, 1933, Utah became the thirty-sixth state to ratify the Twenty-First Amendment, which brought Prohibition to an end, most of the country heaved a sigh of relief. The neighborhood tavern and the more elegant cocktail lounge now replaced the speakeasy. No longer did one have to depend on a password to quench his thirst.

Stewart Warner Radio. Billboard, c. 1930. Collection of Business Americana, Smithsonian Institution.

In the mid-twenties, two uniquely different entertainment media emerged simultaneously. Although radio and the movies had been invented earlier—the 1920 presidential election had been broadcast on the radio, and films were being screened in American cities as early as 1896—it took the post-World War I economy to give both the push they needed. Radio eventually became a star salesman for thousands of mass-produced products, and film has had a penetrating and lasting effect on tastes and fashions.

The wartime period had marked the transformation of the motion picture from a spectacle for the poor into a major form of middle-class entertainment. Following the war, movies became the newest major industry in the United States. The twenties witnessed the rise of the movie star as a middle-class cult figure who had strong influence on American tastes and fashions. John Barrymore, Rudolph Valentino, Gloria Swanson, Pola Negri, and other idols of the silver screen lived in fabulous Hollywood mansions and were driven about in chauffeured limousines. Producers had enormous investments riding on each picture and counted on the stars to draw the public.

Most directors were little known, but Cecil B. de Mille achieved prominence for his historical epics and his celebration of Jazz Age hedonism. In a series of films, de Mille condoned the new morality, the flouting of conventions, and the relentless pursuit of pleasure. He fabricated a collective sex fantasy out of luxurious boudoirs and elegant women *en déshabillé*.

The male counterpart of de Mille's sex idol was Rudolph Valentino, whose torrid love scenes, particularly in *The Sheik*, made women scream. Millions of people attended local theaters weekly, particularly after the stock market crashed. Manufacturers were quick to seize on any new trends and styles that they could glean from the films and developed products to satisfy an avid public.

While the motion picture was at the height of its popularity, another entertainment medium was suffering from underuse. The sale of phonograph records had fallen from 107 million discs in 1927 to only 6 million in 1932. Once the radio and record player were sold in the same cabinet, however, record sales revived. In the forties, when radio began to feature recorded music played by a disc jockey rather than broadcasting live bands as it had in earlier decades, records were once again a hot item.

Although liquor wasn't sold legally in the 1920s, cigarettes were available in abundance and were promoted in brash ad campaigns. During World War I, millions of soldiers had begun to smoke cigarettes. Cigarette purchases, which accounted for only 5 percent of tobacco sales in 1904, soon

Top: Chesterfield Cigarettes. Poster, c. 1917. Metropolitan Museum of Art. The flying ace, a World War I hero, was identified with Chesterfield. Illustration by J. C. Leyendecker. Bottom: Early Camel advertising was naive.

overtook cigars and pipe tobacco. In the 1920s, there were thousands of cigarette brands, most of which were distributed locally.

The leading cigarette in the 1920s and 1930s was an R. J. Reynolds brand called Camels. In 1920, George Washington Hill became president of the American Tobacco Company and devoted the major part of his advertising budget to overtaking Camels. Hill decided to pit a little known brand called Lucky Strike against the leader. Together with advertising genius Albert J. Lasker, Hill made a strong pitch to women, for whom smoking was considered undignified and sinful. In 1919, Murad and Helmer brand cigarettes had shown women in their advertising, but the women pictured were Oriental houris clad in exotic garb. Mythical ladies of pleasure could smoke a Murad, but not the girl next door. Chesterfield broke the barrier against representing women in cigarette advertising with their 1926 billboard showing a man and woman seated on a moonlit riverbank. The man was lighting up; the woman was coaxing him to "blow some my way." There was a tremendous public outcry against this billboard, but it cleared the way for "closet" smokers to puff in public without violating social mores. Lasker and Hill changed the smoking habits of the entire female population of the United States. Lasker used many celebrities along with singers from the Metropolitan Opera Company to testify in advertisements that they smoked Lucky Strikes to protect their voices. The head of the International Society for Christian Endeavor warned that "womanhood is being exploited for trade," but Hill and Lasker forged ahead, coming up with one brilliant slogan after another.

One of Lasker's copywriters is said to have received a ten-thousand-dollar bonus for coming up with the slogan, "So round, so firm, so fully packed, so free and easy on the draw." The sexual overtones were thinly veiled and testified to the libertine atmosphere of the 1920s. Eventually, Luckies came to be so well known that an acronym, "LS/MFT"— "Lucky Strike Means Fine Tobacco"—was sufficient to identify the brand. In the late 1920s, Lucky Strikes were outselling their competitors, including the brand touted by the midget bellhop who proclaimed, "Call for Philip Morris," to make cigarette smoking by both sexes acceptable and even desirable.

The soap manufacturers were as busy as the tobacco companies in expanding their market. They identified women as a separate consumer class to whom special appeals could be directed. Since soap advertisers perceived women as primarily concerned with being beautiful, socially acceptable, staying young, and attracting men, they promoted their products as the means of satisfying these aims.

Top: Ivory Soap. Billboard, c. 1924. Private collection. Courtesy of Procter & Gamble. Center: Ivory Soap. Billboard, c. 1924. Private collection. Courtesy of Procter & Gamble. Bottom: Ivory Soap. Billboard, c. 1924. Private collection. Courtesy of Procter & Gamble. During the '20s, Ivory Soap intensified its advertising showing beautiful women enjoying the good life.

The only claim not made for soaps was that they had cleaning power. Woodbury's glamour campaign of the 1920s promised women "The Skin You Love to Touch." Palmolive became the leading beauty soap in the world with advertisements featuring beautiful women with "schoolgirl complexions." One of the awesome discoveries of the 1920s was body odor, really an invention of Lever Brothers, whose Lifebuoy soap promised to rid users of the horrible "B.O." that made one a social outcast. Lever Brothers did much to create a style of ad copy with phrases like, "Lifebuoy's antiseptic lather." The public was told that "Lifebuoy penetrates each pore and removes every trace of odor-causing waste." "The soap," said Lever, was "not a substitute for cleanliness but cleanliness itself." Soon toothpastes were offering matchless smiles, deodorants were staving off underarm perspiration, and mouthwash was doing combat with bad breath.

The sophisticated advertising campaigns of the twenties made purchasing a means of satisfying one's sense of well-being in addition to providing for one's needs. In support of advertising's benefits, Bruce Barton, one of the leading advertising figures of the 1920s, wrote a 1925 bestseller, *The Man Nobody Knows*, in which he declared that Jesus Christ, "would be a national advertiser today . . . as he was the greatest advertiser of his own day."

Advertising agencies rose to positions of great influence as manufacturers' advertising budgets ballooned. Art directors and copywriters, taking their cues from the times, used more provocative pictures and copy. The profession also turned its knowledge of selling products to selling itself. In a magazine campaign in the mid-twenties, a little guy called Andy Consumer said, "I begin to see that it's advertising that makes America hum. It gives ginks like me a goal. Makes us want something. And the world is so much the better for our heaving a little harder."

A sales technique that became prominent in the twenties was testimonial advertising. Beginning with soaps, lotions, and breakfast foods, it came to be used for scores of other commodities. Celebrities of all types—opera singers, prizefighters, movie stars, baseball players, explorers—were all available for the right price. The celebrity became a new kind of folk hero. It was he whom middle-class Americans now wished to emulate rather than the aristocrats of Park Avenue and Newport, who had formerly been America's tastemakers.

The shift away from emulation of the aristocracy was due to a number of factors. The "upper-crust" preferred a low profile and did not wish its tastes or lifestyle to be publicized. Conversely, celebrities courted the media and made their tastes, opinions, and even the photos of interiors

Kuppenheimer. Store poster, c. 1923. Collection of Business Americana, Smithsonian Institution. Illustration by J. C. Leyendecker.

of their homes available to the public. As the business structure solidified, the Horatio Alger myth faded away and an aristocratic life achieved by business success seemed inaccessible to most people. The celebrity, however, was likely to have been someone of humble origins who had gained status by some special talent that could be found among all classes.

Agents put together lists of celebrities who would endorse anything for a fee. People who could hardly write their names swore they used only a specific pen. Movie stars often lent their names to as many as fifty or sixty products.

Charles Lindbergh, who made the first solo flight across the Atlantic Ocean on May 20, 1927, became an instant celebrity, and manufacturers clamored for his endorsement. He testified to the excellence of the Parker fountain pen, which he said he carried with him on his flight. The manufacturers of the steel used in building the *Spirit of St. Louis*, the makers of the spark plugs in its engines, and the refiners of the oil it burned all told the public how their products had contributed to the success of the flight. The world-famous Dionne quintuplets earned about half a million dollars endorsing a variety of products. Their pictures appeared on a Quaker oats poster, among others. When they were only two years old, they told the public, through words put in their mouths by an advertising copywriter, that it should use only one soap for sensitive skins, the one made with "gentle" olive oil.

Testimonial advertising was misused extensively before the twenties ended, but there was no outcry from the public, which liked to be identified with the glamorous figures. In the 1970s, the Federal Trade Commission, objected to the use of testimonials unless the ads containing them stated that a fee had been paid to the endorser whose name was used. The Federal Trade Commission has since had more experience with "truth in advertising" cases, and it now prosecutes companies with dubious advertising practices. The recent controversy over whether Bruce Jenner, the Olympic decathlon star who endorsed Wheaties, actually did eat the cereal as a child is a case in point. Jenner and Wheaties escaped expensive litigation only when they were able to demonstrate that Wheaties had indeed been a part of the athlete's diet when he was a growing boy.

The testimonial as well as the billboard was a powerful sales effort which became widespread after World War I. Billboards were clustered near intersections in the cities and along the growing number of highways in the countryside. Such artists as Maxfield Parrish and J. C. Leyendecker, both of whom survived the transition from the art posters of the 1890s to the demands of twentieth-century commerce, received more exposure than ever before. Parrish

Arrow Collars and Shirts. Billboard. c. 1922. Private collection. Courtesy of Arrow Shirt Company, a division of Cluett, Peabody and Company. J. C. Leyendecker's Arrow Man guides a lovely lady around the dance floor.

brought a world of fairy-tale charm and fantasy to the roadways. His billboard series for Fisk tires was filled with characters who seemed to have stepped out of *Mother Goose*.

J. C. Leyendecker's best-known posters and billboards were for Chesterfield cigarettes and Cluett & Peabody's Arrow shirts and collars. Leyendecker was the creator of the handsome Arrow man, who looked like a character from *The Great Gatsby*. The Arrow man's sophistication was much admired by women in the twenties. He was suave, worldly wise, and possessed a kind of "cool" associated today with more rugged types like the Marlboro man. The Arrow man, created as a product trademark, became a middle-class culture hero.

Billboard and poster artists in the twenties portrayed Americans as they wished they could be. Fantasy and reality were mingled in a modern dreamworld where the inhabitants had an attractiveness or sense of well-being that always seemed just beyond the grasp of the average person.

Illustration dominated commercial art in America before World War II. The sweeping changes in European design gradually filtered across the Atlantic, but were adopted only by the most progressive artists and manufacturers. Cubism, Futurism, de Stijl, Constructivism, and other art movements had radically altered graphic design in Europe. Since the turn of the century artists like Lucien Bernhard and Ludwig Hohlwein in Germany and A. M. Cassandre, Jean Carlu, and Paul Colin in France had continued the tradition of fine art posters for advertising. In Berlin, Bernhard had created spectacular posters for Stiller Shoes, Manoli Cigarettes, and Priester Matches. Cassandre's posters for the European railroads and steamship lines embodied a strong sense of movement, tasteful typography, and elegant design.

The rectilinear lines and stylized illustration of art deco had some influence on American magazine and poster advertising of the 1920s and 1930s, particularly in the fashion industry, where the merchandise had to reflect contemporary styles.

Much of the outdoor advertising in America was on large twenty-four-sheet billboards, while the small poster was still the primary form of public communication in Europe. American billboard illustration evolved to fit the medium at hand. The graphic subtleties of a Cassandre poster, so effective on a Paris kiosk, would have been lost on a billboard that had to be viewed at a distance from a moving vehicle.

Most of the American billboard artists of the twenties are little known today. Clarence G. Underwood popularized the Palmolive woman with the "schoolgirl complexion." Charles E. Chambers did many of the Chesterfield boards.

"Realistic pictures of people are what most people understand," he said. "That may be because people visualize themselves doing what life-like characters are doing, and cannot identify themselves with less real figures." Norman Rockwell, so closely identified with the *Saturday Evening Post* for many years, also did occasional billboards. Other artists who created advertising billboards and posters before World War II were Burr Griffin, who was responsible for the sleepy towheaded Fisk tire boy, Fred Cooper, and Adolph Treidler.

*Poster Advertising, Billboard, c. 1927.
Private collection.*

The size of the billboard changed the means of reproducing the billboard image. A twenty-four-sheet billboard poster was too large to be lithographed. Instead, the design had to be photographed in color and enlarged many times. The development of the photo-offset printing process at the end of the nineteenth century made the reproduction of photographs possible. Photographs, which now dominate outdoor advertising, were not widely used for billboards until the 1940s. Among the earliest billboard photographs were advertisements designed for magazine display that had been enlarged to billboard proportions. Today, magazine advertisements and billboards that are part of the same campaign can look different from one another. An exception is the recent Cutty Sark campaign, which features a gigantic blowup of part of the Cutty label on both the billboards and in magazines.

The electric sign was another type of outdoor advertising that grew rapidly after World War I. It was preceded by gaslit signs as early as the 1840s; notable among them was P. T. Barnum's huge sign for his museum, which lit up Broadway for several blocks. Drugstores, tobacco shops, and barrooms were the leaders in the use of gaslit outdoor signs.

The first electric sign appeared in New York on Broadway in 1891. A number of these signs, which far exceeded the twenty-four-sheet billboards in size, were in place around Broadway and Twenty-third Street by 1893, giving Broadway the name the Great White Way. Amusements and newspapers were the first users of the new medium. An early electric sign sixty feet wide and thirty feet high proclaimed that the New York *World* had a circulation of over five million copies a week. One of the first manufacturers to advertise with the giant electric signs was the H. J. Heinz Company. The fifty-foot Heinz sign atop the Flatiron Building featured an enormous pickle with green bulbs and the name *Heinz* across it in white. Beneath the pickle, huge letters, composed of electric bulbs, spelled out the names of Heinz's 57 Varieties. The Heinz sign became known throughout the country as a successful demonstration of the wonders of electricity for advertising and spurred other manufacturers to make use of the medium.

O. J. Gude, who became known as the Father of the Great White Way, was the man behind the spread of electric signs in New York. From Broadway and Twenty-third Street, he moved farther north until his displays reached Times Square. In 1910, the Rice Electrical Display Company built an electric sign seven stories high on the roof of the Hotel Normandie overlooking Herald Square in order to induce manufacturers to use its services. Twenty thousand electric bulbs of various colors flashed twenty-five hundred times a minute to display the movement of a giant Roman chariot race with the chariot drivers whipping their galloping horses at a furious pace. This feat was outdone several years later by the famous Wrigley's Spearmint sign at Times Square. It was two hundred feet long by fifty feet high. The little spearmen, a logo for Wrigley's gum, were fifteen feet high. The tails of the exquisite peacocks at the top of the sign were sixty feet long and the spouting fountains at either end were thirty-four feet high.

The technology of electric signs eventually developed to include the giant electric screens with changing patterns of lights that give the appearance of an animated film. Another variation on the billboard was the Brobdingnagian sign depicting a smoker from whose mouth huge gusts of smoke billowed.

The proliferation of enormous electric signs throughout the twenties was indicative of an expansive economy. Then, on October 29, 1929, the stock market crashed. In the late twenties there had been widespread optimism about the future of the market. Thousands were pouring money into stocks without looking too closely at the earnings of the companies in which they were investing. Stock prices soared. Overblown prospectuses, unhampered by federal regulation, promised quick profits for unsuspecting investors. During the market's tailspin, over thirty billion dollars had disappeared before order was restored in mid-November. This amount exceeded the national debt.

At first the economy did not seem gravely affected, but ebbing sales, salary cuts, and layoffs eventually spelled disaster. Banks closed in increasing numbers. In 1929, 659 banks closed their doors, affecting 230 million dollars in deposits. The following year, 1,352 banks suspended operation, tying up 853 million dollars in savings. In 1931, the number of banks that closed rose to 2,294, representing a staggering 1,690,669,000 dollars in lost deposits. President Hoover convened a series of White House conferences of businessmen to devise a plan for dealing with the disaster, but he was hampered by his dogged faith in the private sector's ability to confront its problems and by his own reluctance to marshall the full weight of government to solve them.

Chesterfield Cigarettes. Streetcar poster, c. 1944. Collection of Vivian and Ira Brichta.

WORLD WAR II

The world found a cure for its economic depression, but the cure was more painful than the disease. It was World War II.

During Franklin Delano Roosevelt's first term in office, the United States began to build and equip a peacetime army with modern planes, tanks, ammunition, uniforms, and food. Industries that were awarded government defense contracts reduced America's eight million unemployed to five and one-half million by 1942. As another war in Europe became inevitable, defense contracts continued to proliferate and those Depression survivors still unemployed dwindled to a few hundred thousand. After more than a decade of severe depression labor and industry responded with record-breaking energy to the new war effort.

Producers of war materials didn't worry too much about costs. Orders were placed on the basis of how many and how fast, and the government paid the bills. Automakers built tanks and ships, a well-known lipstick manufacturer produced bullet casings, and clothing manufacturers turned out GI regulation uniforms by the thousands daily. Huge numbers of American men were called into service, and women took over many jobs formerly held by men.

Refrigerators, cars, and furniture wore out and were im-

By 1932, industry was operating at less than half its maximum 1929 volume. In the same year, the total amount paid in wages was 60 percent less than it had been in 1929. People coped as best they could. Some moved to rural areas where they could at least live off the land. In the cities, breadlines lengthened. Sidewalk soup kitchens doled out a meager sustenance to the hungry. Stores closed, and beggars and panhandlers were very much in evidence. The relief rolls swelled until they included eighteen million people, and the police were apprehensive about potential violence. Men sold apples and pencils on street corners to survive. On vacant lots outside the cities, Hoovervilles—groups of tarpaper shacks—named with intentional irony after President Hoover sheltered people who had lost their homes..

Franklin D. Roosevelt's New Deal addressed the problems more squarely than Hoover had. On March 12, 1932, President Roosevelt, during the first hundred days of his administration, delivered one of his "fireside chats" to the public, assuring them that measures had been taken to strenghten the banks and urging them to redeposit their money. The appeal was so convincing that panic runs on the banks ceased despite the fact that no actual guarantee of solvency had been given. The creation of the Federal Deposit Insurance Corporation followed in 1933; this represented a federal guarantee to the savings of small depositors in full and of large depositors in part.

The Depression confirmed the need for some government involvement in the nation's economic life, both in its regulatory aspects and in the girding of banking institutions. The New Deal, devised to combat the Depression, created thousands of badly needed jobs through massive work programs such as the Civilian Conservation Corps, which employed three hundred thousand young men to work on soil conservation and forest protection projects, and the Work Projects Administration, which, among other things, employed large numbers of artists to paint murals in public buildings and record America's folklore. The WPA Poster Project adopted contemporary European styles at a time when few manufacturers were interested in them. The WPA posters promoted the activities of public agencies, announced safety rules, encouraged domestic tourism, and gave advice on everything from nutrition to prenatal care. The use of modern graphics was the contribution of Richard Floethe, the director of the project, who had studied at the Bauhaus and was dedicated to strong, contemporary design.

Owing to financial pressures, industry became more efficient and important technological advances occurred. The idea of product research and development was formulated during this period. Cellophane revolutionized pack-

aging; freon refrigerant improved the cold storage of food; plastics of all kinds were introduced; and nylon stockings and lingerie altered women's fashions.

Advertising, which was riding high in the twenties, suffered a severe attack during the Depression years. To the degree that it was linked to business and industry, it was accused of holding out false promises. It had been allegedly used to urge people to buy things they couldn't afford and to want things they couldn't have. The attack differed from that waged earlier in the century against false claims and overblown promises. This time the entire economic system was being criticized. In 1932, F. J. Schlink and Arthur Kellet, officials of Consumer's Research, Inc., a leading consumer organization, published *100,000,000 Guinea Pigs*, a best-seller that bitterly assailed all advertising. In the best tradition of yellow journalism, it was a list of lurid crimes. The public, glad to find a scapegoat for its woes, didn't question the authors' facts nor did it realize that many of the cases of adulteration, misrepresentation, or quackery cited were decades old and that few of the practices mentioned were typical of reputable national advertisers. The book was so successful that it engendered a succession of imitators. These books pilloried Henry Ford, General Motors, Coca-Cola, canned foods, and the drug industry in toto. The only positive result of the antiadver-

possible to replace since consumer products requiring strategic war materials for their manufacture were not being made. Bobby pins, razor blades, and small appliances were highly prized possessions, and patriotic citizens saved metal and old newspapers for the scrap drives. For a time, one could not purchase a tube of toothpaste without first returning a used tube to the storekeeper.

Sugar, meats, and canned goods were rationed, as was gasoline. For the most part, people cooperated and traded ration stamps for price-controlled products. A few, however, created a black market that extended well beyond the war years. "How much under the table?" became a stock question while negotiating for anything from rentable apartments to steaks. Those ready to pay usually got what they wanted.

When Germany and Japan capitulated, factories that were fulfilling war contracts switched to consumer products. Postwar goods and services were much in demand by millions of Americans who had saved their earnings during the war years to help finance a comfortable peacetime existence.

Unlike the end of World War I, which heralded a national recession, the end of World War II began a boom in business, babies, and education.

tising movement was the formation of the Consumer's Union. Through its publication *Consumer Reports*, which publishes detailed evaluations of all major products, the organization has for many years provided a valuable service to the consumer.

Some of President Roosevelt's chief advisors, notably Rexford Tugwell, had little good to say about advertising. Tugwell drafted a bill that, if passed, would have given the federal government greatly increased powers to regulate the advertising and manufacturing industries. The Tugwell bill was defeated in congress, but that did not prevent the Federal Trade Commission, whose powers were broadened in 1938 by the passage of the Wheeler-Lee Amendment, from prohibiting the dissemination of false or misleading advertising, or from issuing injunctions against a number of companies for violations of the amendment.

When the United States entered World War II, the government resolved that American troops would be the best equipped in history. Industry, in spite of reduced production during the Depression, was well prepared for the war effort. The need for more efficient means of production in the thirties had increased the output per man hour by a whopping 41 percent during the decade 1930–1940; this compared with only 21 percent during the expansion of the twenties and only 7 percent between 1910 and 1920, the period that included World War I. The ambitious job of military production was accomplished by turning out what was required as quickly as possible and paying little attention to costs. New plants were built in a hurry and old ones were converted to military production. The entire automobile industry was diverted to the production of tanks, trucks, and weapons; typewriter manufacturers made machine gun parts. With the application of new techniques of research and development, many new products and devices were produced. These ranged from synthetic rubber to radar, from proximity fuses to penicillin and DDT. The most complex and costly research project in history, the Manhattan Project, marshalled the skills of thousands of scientists to produce the atomic bomb.

The result of all this feverish activity was a boost of the GNP in 1945 to $215 billion, several times greater than the $91 billion of 1939. By 1943, the unemployment of the Depression years had virtually disappeared. The principal beneficiaries were workers in the war industries. People were lured from other jobs by salaries two and three times higher than what they had been making. Women who did not work before were urged to take factory jobs to ease the manpower shortage. Rosie the Riveter, with her overalls and a kerchief tied around her head, was a familiar figure on the home front. During the war, industry achieved the most spectacular increase in production that had ever been accomplished in any five-year period of economic history. American families suddenly found themselves prosperous but had little on which to spend their money. No automobiles were being made; food, clothing, and gasoline were rationed; and other products were generally scarce. Despite the shortages and scarcities, there was a resurgence of advertising during World War II. Advertisers had learned from the previous war that it was valuable to keep their brand names before the public even when their products weren't available. Besides, advertising was cheap in wartime since the Department of the Treasury allowed a reasonable amount of advertising as a legitimate business expense.

The wartime situation varied from company to company. Manufacturers of cosmetics and some manufacturers of prepared and canned foods and tobacco could carry on business as usual. Others, whose plants were entirely devoted to the production of military equipment or supplies, could not. These included the entire automobile industry and its subsidiary suppliers of parts, as well as manufacturers of farm implements, appliances, and other consumer durables. Much advertising was institutional. Some manufacturers could honestly point to their contributions to the war effort; others, whose contributions were tenuous or nil, found other ways to show that they were helping to win the war.

National manufacturers often worked war themes into their regular advertising. B. F. Goodrich, urging people to conserve tires, declared "Hitler Smiles When You Waste Miles." The Pabst Brewing Company proposed a toast: "To the Jap Navy—Bottoms Up." Green Giant peas told people how to grow peas in their victory gardens and Bell Telephone urged phone users to stay off the long-distance wires so servicemen could get their calls through.

Generally agencies cooperated with the Office of War Information and with a group of advertisers and agency personnel called the War Advertising Council. Advertising was effective in keeping the war in the public consciousness and supporting the home-front effort. The techniques used were more sophisticated than they had been in World War I when radio was unavailable, photography little used, and copy lengthy. In both wars, unfortunately, lurid racial stereotypes were used to represent the enemy and scare tactics were employed to boost production.

When the war ended, signs of prosperity were everywhere. Long hours of factory overtime had fattened millions of pay envelopes and savings accounts. Vast numbers were lifted into a secure position in the middle class. They had lots of money, and a sophisticated industrial system was gearing up to help them spend it.

BURMA SHAVE

Something—or somebody—
killed it.

It was either the advent of
the expressway and high-speed
cars or the development of the
electric razor, or perhaps it
was the fact that Philip Morris
bought the company in 1964.
In any event, Burma Shave
died; died right there on the
American highway where it
was born in 1927.

Burma Shave used eighteen-
by-forty-inch boards spaced
about one hundred feet apart
along the highway to advertise
their shaving cream. A family
driving by at thirty-five miles
per hour had three seconds to
read each of the six signs dis-
playing the jingle. Thousands
of kids learned speed reading
while out in the old Ford on a
Sunday afternoon.

The answer to
a maiden's
prayer
is not a chin
of stubby hair
Burma Shave

In the 1930s and 1940s,
highways were a lot different
than they are today; two
lanes, one in each direction,
were standard. Farmers whose
property bordered on roads
were grateful for the extra income the signs provided.
Burma Shave crews followed
each other around the country,
one group negotiating with
farmers for the placement of
jingle signs on their property
while the second crew constructed and placed the signs.
During the thirty years that
Burma Shave flourished, dozens of such crews dotted highways from coast to coast,
scouting, installing, repairing,
and changing jingle signs.

By 1940, as Burma Shave
gained momentum and its distribution increased, over forty
thousand invididual signs were
in position. And every sign, every crew, every deal made with
each farmer was recorded in
the computerlike mind of Fidelia
Dearlove.

Fidelia worked as a secre-
tary for the owners of the
Burma Shave Company, Leonard and Allan Odell. While the
Odells were changing the na-

Their First Ride

tion's shaving habits from lathering-up with a mug and brush to using a brushless shaving cream, Fidelia Dearlove kept track of the special Burma Shave trucks, each with the words "Cheer up" emblazoned on its side panel, and she knew by heart where every jingle was located.

Few American advertisers ever received as much acceptance for their ads as did Burma Shave. Alexander Wolcott said it was as difficult to eat one salted peanut as it was to read one Burma Shave sign.

The spacing of the signs enforced a particular reading pace, and what suspense! Even the most alert passenger could not read ahead to the punch line; everyone in the car read and enjoyed it simultaneously.

Beneath this stone
lies Elmer Gush,
tickled to death
by his
shaving brush.
Burma Shave

Whether it was due to the expressways, the advent of electronic advertising, or more sophisticated marketing, the Burma Shave road signs are gone. But buried with each sign is a brief yet memorable part of poster advertising in America.

Farewell O'Verse
Along the road
How sad to
Know you're
Out of Mode
Burma Shave

Opposite, top: Overland Motor Car. Showroom poster, c. 1915. Metropolitan Museum of Art. In 1907, The Knox Waterless Limousine could be left outside in the coldest weather and would still start without trouble. The Knox was equipped with imported goat skin upholstery and a speaking tube for passengers to communicate with the driver. In 1912 the Interstate Auto proclaimed itself the "automobile for women" because it had home-styled electric lights. Overland in 1915 was going after the farm market. And because of a gas shortage during World War I, the Doble Detroit Steam Car ran on Kerosene. Opposite, bottom: Marathon Lager Beer. Sign, c. 1940. Collection of Vivian and Ira Brichta. Before testimonials by athletes were big business, a ball player might have received $5 or $10 to have his picture identified with a product. Above: Bella Mundo Cigars. Window sign, 16" × 20", c. 1900. Collection of Vivian and Ira Brichta. The American beauty with ankles showing sold 5¢ cigars at a baseball game.

Kirschbaum Clothes. Poster, c. 1912. Collection of Vivian and Ira Brichta. American travelers: an appeal to the wealthy.

LUCKY STRIKE AND CIGARETTES

The Duke family resurrected the name of an old plug chewing tobacco, *Lucky Strike.* Soon after Buck Duke, son of the founder, died, an entrepreneur named George Washington Hill took over Duke's American Tobacco Company. Hill was something of a gambler, an innovative merchandiser, and a very colorful character. The book and subsequent film, *The Hucksters,* both issued in the fifties, was loosely based on his career.

Hill believed in the magic of the Lucky Strike name and gambled his entire advertising budget on that one brand, a risky approach to mass selling. His showmanship, along with the genius of Albert J. Lasker, who was responsible for the advertising success of products such as Pepsodent, Kleenex, Quaker Oats, and Frigidaire, helped catapult Lucky Strike into position as one of the leading brands on the market. It was Lasker's firm that created the phrase, "Reach for a Lucky instead of a sweet," and who secured Lucky Strike testimonials from several of the leading actresses of the day along with aviation heroine Amelia Earhart. Lucky Strike posters were everywhere. "Your Hit Parade" sponsored by The American Tobacco Company was the leading radio, and later television, program for a quarter of a century.

During World War II, Hill

Top: Virginia Cigarettes. Window sign, 20" × 24", c. 1940. Collection of Vivian and Ira Brichta. Bottom: Old North State Cigarettes. Store sign, 12" × 16", c. 1920. Collection of Vivian and Ira Brichta. Listerine, Rum and Maple, Coffee Time, Airline, Twenty Grand, Spud, Wings, Home Runs, Sunshine: cigarette brands proliferated as competition for "smokes" at 10¢ per package intensified.

Top: Campbell's Soups. Billboard, c. 1930. Metropolitan Museum of Art. Grace Gebbie Drayton created The Campbell Kids in 1904. The jovial cartoon children graced one of the longest-running advertising campaigns in the food industry. Bottom: Royal Tailors. Sign and catalog page, c. 1920. Collection of Vivian and Ira Brichta. Enlarged catalog pages hung as broadsides were used by clothing manufacturers to sell to retailers.

cashed in on the fact that the green ink used to print the face of the Lucky Strike package was in short supply. He came up with the slogan "Lucky Strike green has gone to war," changed the color of the package to white, and the sale of Lucky's increased yet another 40 percent—Lucky Strike became the country's largest selling brand of cigarettes.

Prior to 1929, cigarette smoking had been identified with men in most posters. If used in ads at all, women were nonsmoking models, since it was not considered good manners for women to smoke in public or at parties. A woman was arrested in New York City for smoking in the back seat of an automobile in 1904, and, even after World War I, dancer Irene Castle caused a sensation when she lit a cigarette in the public dining room of a hotel.

The cigarette industry has gone through many changes. In 1895, cigarette smoking waned, not as a result of warnings on packages or reports of diseases from use, but because of taxation. Before taxes were added to the price, a smoker could buy a package of Vanity Fair, Golden Age, Estrella, or Cloth of Gold for a nickel. With taxes, the price of cigarettes almost doubled, and splendidly named brands, such as Bon-Tons, Opera Puffs, and Sweet Caporals, were forced out of the market.

PROHIBITION

At 12:01 A.M. on December 5, 1933, the most crime-ridden chapter in America's history ended. On that day, Prohibition was officially over and Repeal began. Beer, whiskey, and wine once again flowed legally from coast to coast.

Thirteen years earlier, with the promise of "no more drunkenness, no more jails, and no more wasted lives," the fundamentalist "Drys" won over the "Wets" and the law limiting the use of liquor was put into effect. Although bathtub gin and backyard stills flourished, particularly in rural areas, such home operations produced only small amounts of liquor. They were no match for the multimillion-dollar business organized by gangsters to bring liquor into the country illegally.

In order to stay in business, the Miller Brewing Company in Milwaukee marketed cereal beverages, malt tonic, malt syrup, and carbonated soda drinks. Falstaff in St. Louis sold soft drinks, near beer, hams, and bacon. Speakeasies and hip flasks became as much a part of life during the twenties as did gang wars. The notoriety of Al Capone and his "gangster city," Chicago, spread around the world.

Finally the government recognized that even the most extraordinary efforts of the FBI could not contain the flourishing bootlegging business. Under pressure from the states that sorely missed the millions of dollars once collected from taxing alcoholic beverages, Prohibition was repealed.

Top: Gund's Peerless Beverages. Poster triptych, 48" × 36", c. 1921. Collection of the Gund family. With Prohibition came dozens of liquorless concoctions designed by breweries in their efforts to stay in business. Bottom: Remington Typewriters. Metal sign, c. 1908. Library of Congress. During the 1970s, the Olivetti Company created "The Olivetti Girl." Remington had used the same campaign sixty years earlier.

Top: Jantzen. Billboard, c. 1939. Institute of Outdoor Advertising. The Jantzen trademark, updated through the years, used as a poster illustration during the '20s. Left: Jantzen. Billboard, c. 1925. Private collection.

ATWATER KENT

RADIO

RADIO

"Lux Presents Hollywood."

"Who's that little chatterbox, the one with pretty auburn locks? . . ."

"Who knows what evil lurks in the hearts of men? . . ."

During the 1930s, radio became the most significant form of mass communication and entertainment that man had ever known. The airways brought news, music, and drama into every home via Philco, RCA, Atwater Kent, Stewart Warner, and Erla radio sets. A new presence of sound that titillated the imagination was available at the flick of a switch. People were talking about the certain death of the newspapers and magazines. Even books were being threatened. Who needed the printed page when there was radio?

Americans owned more radios than bathtubs, and they listened eagerly to programs such as "The A & P Gypsies," "The Happiness Boys," and "The Rudy Vallee Show." Some of the voices that invaded Depression homes belonged to Burns and Allen, Jack Benny, Edgar Bergen and Charlie McCarthy, and Bing Crosby.

Top: Atwater Kent. Billboard, c. 1927. Private collection. Bottom: Uneeda Biscuit. Streetcar poster, c. 1925. Collection of Vivian and Ira Brichta. Words were not necessary to express the appeal of this product.

THE NATIONAL SODA CRACKER
Uneeda Biscuit

SOLD ONLY IN PACKAGES

5¢

IN ER SEAL

Uneeda Biscuit

NATIONAL BISCUIT COMPANY

Uneeda Biscuit. Eight-sheet poster, c. 1912. Collection of Vivian and Ira Brichta. Early in the century, Uneeda launched the first million-dollar ad campaign in history. As the biscuits moved from the cracker barrel to the grocer's shelves, sales skyrocketed.

UNIVERSAL PERCOLATOR

Extracts the Full Flavor and Aroma From Each Grain of Coffee

The UNIVERSAL Gives You Better Coffee in the Cup from Less Coffee in the Pot

"Do Your Bit" in the Economy Campaign

Universal Percolator. Store sign, 20" × 24", c. 1918. Collection of Vivian and Ira Brichta. Selling patriotism and percolators together was a neat trick.

Sponsors became identified with particular programs.

Jell-O, Ipana ("For the Kiss of Beauty") and Sal Hepatica ("For the Smile of Health"), all products advertised on radio, became household words. And late afternoon was devoted to children's shows such as "Jack Armstrong—the All-American Boy," "Little Orphan Annie," "The Lone Ranger," and "Renfrew of the Mounties." Wheaties, Ovaltine, and Lava soap sponsored the fifteen-minute or half-hour kiddie "soaps."

Broadcasters Lowell Thomas, H. V. Kaltenborn, and Boake Carter were welcomed nightly into thousands of living rooms. They were much admired for their incisive interpretations of world news, which matched the basic conservative views of most Americans.

During those halcyon days posters were used to advertise radio. "Listen to 'Amos 'n Andy,'" or "Don't miss the 'Jack Benny Show' on Sunday night" were the subjects of posters or were snipes (additions) to existing posters on display in drugstores, groceries, and hardware stores from coast to coast.

CREAM OF WHEAT

The first Cream of Wheat posters appeared around 1896. Cream of Wheat was a small mill in Grand Forks, North Dakota, owned by Emery Mapes.

Mapes was both an art lover and an advertising genius who believed in the drama of the poster. He commissioned the best artists and photographers of his day to help him sell—or rather, undersell—his product. Most of the early Cream of Wheat posters depicted life in the United States. James Montgomery Flagg, Jessie Wilcox, N. C. Wyeth, and Walter Whitehead worked for Cream of Wheat producing wordless illustrations in a soft-sell style. In his early advertisements, Mapes allowed no claims, no inducements to buy, no premiums, and no promises.

Rastus, the smiling black chef, was introduced as the cereal's trademark only when Mapes's entrepreneurial needs to sell finally took precedence over his love of art. Even with Rastus, the Cream of Wheat ads continued to maintain the high level of quality that Emery Mapes had set for the company back before the turn of the century. His contribution to advertising and to the maturing of the professional status of artists who work for advertisers, spanned nearly thirty years, from the middle 1890s through the middle 1920s.

In 1960, when the company was sold, much of its original advertising art was placed in storage. A few years later, fire destroyed it all.

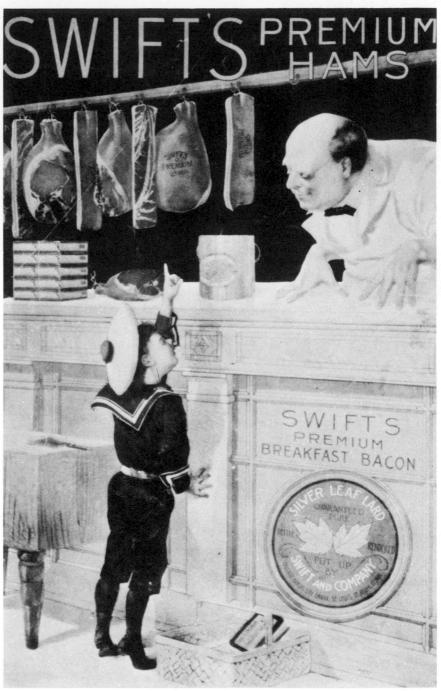

Top, left: Cream of Wheat "Playing Hookey." Poster, 28" × 40", c. 1910. Collection of Vivian and Ira Brichta. The poster of Rastus, the smiling Cream of Wheat chef, serves as a hiding place for Tom and Huck on a day more suitable for fishing than school. Cream of Wheat posters utilized the talents of America's finest artists over the 30-year period when Emery Mapes ran the company. Above: Swift's Premium Hams. Handbill, 9" × 12", c. 1910. Collection of Vivian and Ira Brichta. Courtesy of Swift and Company. In 1855, 16-year-old Gustavus Swift raised a heifer and sold it for a good profit, and Swift was in the cattle business in Chicago.

Top: Reo Speed Wagons. Streetcar poster, c. 1914. Collection of Vivian and Ira Brichta. Just as automobiles changed the American way of life, so did trucks that delivered merchandise to places trains couldn't reach. Rebuilt Reos, paid for on convenient terms, made a lot of sense to the small businessman. Bottom: American Navy Plug Tobacco. Eight-sheet poster, c. 1910. Collection of Vivian and Ira Brichta. The U.S. Navy had successfuly fought a war with Spain. Panama had been created as a result of military action. The threat of war in Europe was a major topic of conversation. Products for men reflected this atmosphere.

BOCK BEER

The Hindustani word for goat is bok.

A Mesopotamian seal from around 2200 B.C. shows a queen and her entourage sipping beer through golden straws . . . and between them a prancing goat.

Some say the word bock comes from the medieval brewing town of Einbeck (pronounced Ein-bock), in Germany.

Whatever the origins of the name, bock beer, advertised on posters for centuries, has rarely been represented without a goat.

Bock is a heavy dark lager beer, traditionally brewed during the winter to be enjoyed in the spring. Americans, however, developed a taste for a sweeter and lighter beer during Prohibition, when soda pop was the only legally available beverage. Faced with the problem of staying in business during the Prohibition era, some breweries developed a "near beer," a nonalcoholic beverage that tasted something like beer. After Prohibition, the heavier European-style beers were the province of serious drinkers while social drinkers preferred lighter beers.

Keep youth's priceless gift—

—that Schoolgirl Complexion

PALMOLIVE

The new Luxury—made of Palm and Olive Oils.

Palmolive
TRADE MARK
the proper thing
For the Bath

Ask your Druggist or Grocer for a Cake!

More precious than jewels

Keep that Schoolgirl Complexion

PALMOLIVE

The Palm and Olive Oil Soap

Top: Billboard. c. 1923. Institute of Outdoor Advertising. Bottom left: Poster. c. 1890. Collection of Vivian and Ira Brichta. Bottom right: Billboard. c. 1925. Institute of Outdoor Advertising.

The "Palmolive Girl with the schoolgirl complexion" belonged to the liberated twenties. She played golf and tennis, rode a horse, and traveled in the desert. Through it all, she had to look "beautiful, charming, delicate, graceful, stylish, and refined." The Palmolive Girl appeared as an infant, a young girl, a mother, and in an obscure stage called "prime-of-life." Whatever her condition, the company decreed her always to be radiant, of good cheer, and eligible for admiring glances.

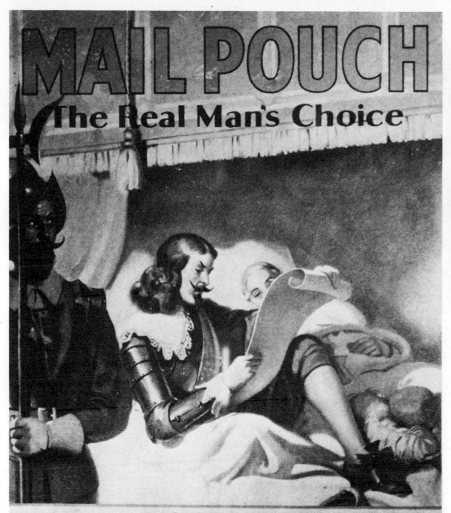

MAIL POUCH
The Real Man's Choice

DIGNITY IN BED

Louis XIII of France carried etiquette to ridiculous extremes. Seeking council of a minister who was too ill to rise, he crawled into bed with him fully clothed. Thus he avoided either standing or sitting while one of lesser rank reclined.

Mail Pouch Smoking Tobacco. Window sign, 16" × 22", c. 1910. Collection of Vivian and Ira Brichta.

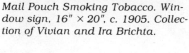

MAIL POUCH
The Real Man's Choice

CACKLING OF GEESE SAVED ROME

When the Gauls swept down on ancient Italy, they attempted to scale the walls of the last stronghold of Rome at night. Tradition tells us that the geese of the temple of Juno were more alert than the defenders and that their warning cackles saved the city.

Mail Pouch Smoking Tobacco. Window sign, 16" × 20", c. 1905. Collection of Vivian and Ira Brichta.

Top: Pears Soap. Poster, 10" × 14", c. 1890. Collection of Vivian and Ira Brichta. Fanciful, delicate illustrations characterized Pears Soap posters. Bottom: Fairy Soap. Handbill, 9" × 12", c. 1900. Collection of Vivian and Ira Brichta.

Star Soap. Poster, 10" × 14", c. 1900. Collection of Vivian and Ira Brichta.

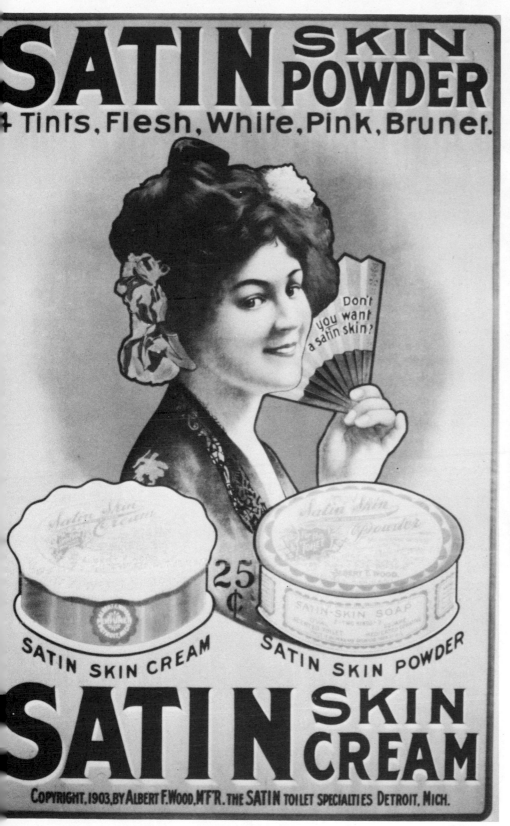

Puritan Tailors. Store sign, 15" × 55", c. 1914. Collection of Vivian and Ira Brichta. A two-button suit with patch pockets; pretty good even by today's standards!

Satin Skin Powder. Window sign, 24" × 36", c. 1900. Collection of Vivian and Ira Brichta. An Oriental influence at the turn of the century.

Top: Flyer Cigars. Store sign, 10" ×
6", c. 1928. Collection of Vivian and
Ira Brichta. Manufacturers climbed on
the Lindbergh bandwagon. Bottom:
Regenburg's Havana Cigars. Sign, 12"
× 18", c. 1930. Collection of Vivian
and Ira Brichta.

Mozart Cigar. Decal on glass, 16" × 20", c. 1915. Collection of Vivian and Ira Brichta.
Famous names like Mozart, Napoleon, and Uncle Sam helped sell cigars and other
products.

NOW AT POPULAR PRICES

Raleigh Cigarettes. Poster, 22" × 28", c. 1940. Collection of Vivian and Ira Brichta. Copyright Brown & Williamson Tobacco Corp. Reprinted with permission; all rights reserved.

Marvel Cigarettes. Store sign, 16" × 20", c. 1940. Collection of Vivian and Ira Brichta.

Red Dot Cigars. Mobile sign, c. 1936. Collection of Vivian and Ira Brichta. Every industry in America felt the effects of the Depression. Cigar manufacturers joined the fight to stay in business by offering twice the quantity at the same 5¢ price.

Top right: Chesterfield Cigarettes. Streetcar cards, c. 1940. Collection of Vivian and Ira Brichta. Fred Waring and Harry James worked for Chesterfield as radio performers. These posters, used as testimonials, were reminders to listen in. Center, right: Target Cigarettes. Streetcar poster, c. 1930. Collection of Vivian and Ira Brichta. The roll-your-own cigarette competed with factory-made brands during the Depression.

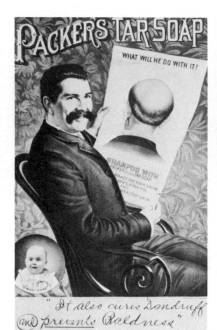

Packers' Tar Soap. Store sign, 10" × 14", c. 1900. Collection of Vivian and Ira Brichta. Still sold today, Packers' advertising claims have been modified.

Bottom, right: White House Coffee. Store sign, 18" × 22", c. 1912. Collection of Vivian and Ira Brichta. A finely detailed illustration of a well-to-do couple. The implication is: Drink White House Coffee and find marital bliss. The same appeal to personal happiness appears in ads today.

The Goodrich Rubber Man's Vacation. Poster, c. 1904. Chicago Historical Society. An early mixture of collage and whimsy to promote automobile tires.

C. Kern Brewing Co. Poster, c. 1910. Library of Congress.

Top: Horton's Perfect 36. Store sign, 48" × 60", c. 1930. Collection of Vivian and Ira Brichta. Washing machines in the '20s and '30s were primarily for city people, since few farmers had running water, sewage disposal, or electricity. Bottom: Lipton's Cocoa. Metal sign, 14" × 18", c. 1929. Collection of Vivian and Ira Brichta. Reprinted with permission of Thomas J. Lipton, Inc. Thomas J. Lipton had ten jobs in three years before he decided that he liked the tea business. By 1910 he owned tea gardens in Sri Lanka and was packaging tea for American and Canadian customers. In the 1920s, the company expanded into other products including cocoa.

Strawbridge & Clothier Shoe Sale. Poster, 20" × 40", c. 1910. Collection of Vivian and Ira Brichta. A Philadelphia department store maintained its image with a dignified woman.

Top, left: M. Hommel Wines. Metal sign, c. 1910. Collection of Vivian and Ira Brichta. Bottom: Christian Diehl Beer. Poster, 20" × 24", c. 1917. Collection of Vivian and Ira Brichta. Prohibition forced the Diehl family to find a new product, evaporated milk. They never returned to their breweries. Top, right: Royal Baking Power. Store sign, c. 1935. Collection of Vivian and Ira Brichta. Courtesy of Standard Brands, Inc. Baking soda and cream of tartar were sold separately until a druggist in Fort Wayne, Indiana, put the two together in 1864 and called his product Royal Baking Powder.

Buffalo Rock Ginger Ale. Lithograph on metal, 12" × 15", c. 1912. Collection of Vivian and Ira Brichta.

Top: Felco Pearls. Store sign, 8" × 10", c. 1910. Collection of Vivian and Ira Brichta. You could tell a lady a mile away by her long pearls and stylish hat. Bottom: Deane's Evening Clothes for Men. Billboard, c. 1929. Institute of Outdoor Advertising. An early European influence on billboard art.

Jacob Hoffman Brewing Company. Poster, 22" × 28", c. 1915. Collection of Vivian and Ira Brichta.

Top: The Centlivre Tonic. Poster, 12" × 20", c. 1912. Collection of Vivian and Ira Brichta. The girl is wearing a World War I nurse's uniform. Bottom: Suffolk Brewery. Poster, 20" × 24", c. 1925. Collection of Vivian and Ira Brichta.

Top: Neuman's Ice Cream. Poster, 40" × 60", c. 1920. Collection of Vivian and Ira Brichta. The name of any manufacturer could be printed on this "blank." Center: Fisk. Billboard, c. 1930. Institute of Outdoor Advertising. An imaginative concept even for contemporary advertising. Bottom: Ti-con-der-oga. Window sign, 16" × 24", c. 1930. Collection of Vivian and Ira Brichta. A subtle history lesson and a handsome design induced storekeepers to put this poster in their windows.

Moxie. Store sign, 10" × 10", c. 1930. Collection of Vivian and Ira Brichta. Moxie is an old brand of soft drink originally called Moxie Nerve Food. Today, the word "moxie" implies audacity.

Welch's. Poster, 20" × 24", c. 1927. Collection of Vivian and Ira Brichta. During the 1930s grape juice was a popular drink. Today orange juice, grapefruit juice, and tomato juice have replaced it in popularity.

Top: Sunoco. Billboard, c. 1940. Institute of Outdoor Advertising. Disney characters were used on posters by advertisers willing to pay the price. Bottom: Cloverbloom Butter. Store sign, 9" × 12", c. 1920. Collection of Vivian and Ira Brichta. Norman Rockwell created the same wholesome characters for posters as he did for The Saturday Evening Post covers.

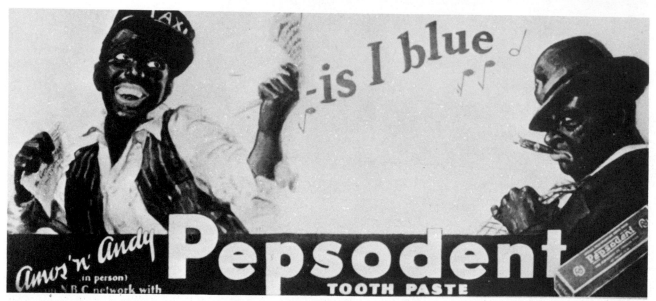

Left: Pioneer Baskets. Store sign, 12"
× 15", c. 1928. Collection of Vivian
and Ira Brichta. Above: Tuttle's Horse
Elixir. Poster, 18" × 24", c. 1905. Collection of Vivian and Ira Brichta.

Mobilgas. Billboard, c. 1940. Institute of Outdoor Advertising. The highly identifiable
flying horse trademark disappeared in the '50s to be replaced by Roman lettering of
the word Mobil.

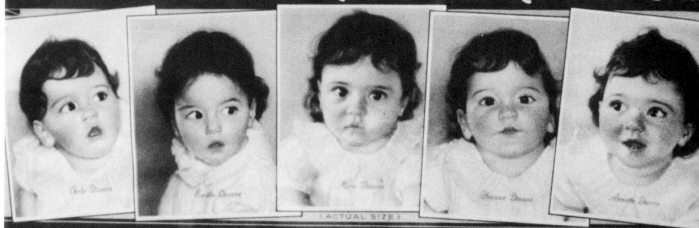

TODAY—THE DIONNE QUINS HAD QUAKER OATS

(ACTUAL SIZE)

FREE! WITH 2 TRADEMARKS FROM QUAKER OR MOTHER'S OATS PACKAGES—ONE OF TH... BEAUTIFUL COLOR PORTRAITS OF YOUR FAVORITE QUIN OR ALL FIVE PICTURES F... 10 TRADEMARKS—SENT WITH COMPLETE DETAILS OF $10,000 DREAM HOME OF... — SEND TO THE QUAKER OATS COMPANY—BOX L—CHICAGO —

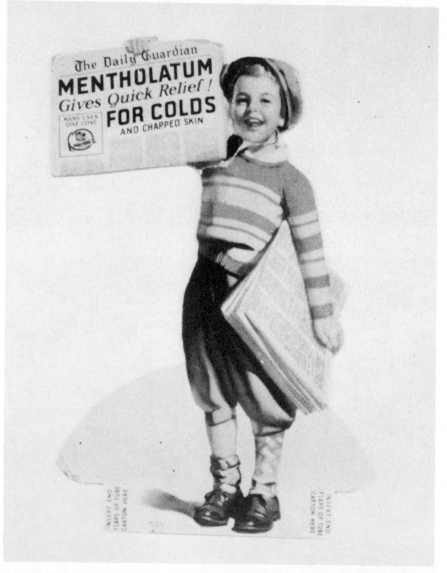

Top: Quaker Oats Company. Dionne quintuplets. Sign. c. 1937. Collection of Vivian and Ira Brichta. Courtesy of Quaker Oats Company. The Dionne family was besieged with offers to have the quintuplets endorse products. Quaker Oats tied their cereal to a most wanted premium: a color photograph of the babies. Bottom: All Star Kola. Poster, 16" × 20". c. 1940. Collection of Vivian and Ira Brichta. The svelte "Petty Girl" influence extended to soft drink advertising as well.

Mentholatum. Store sign. 10" × 8". c. 1930. Collection of Vivian and Ira Brichta.

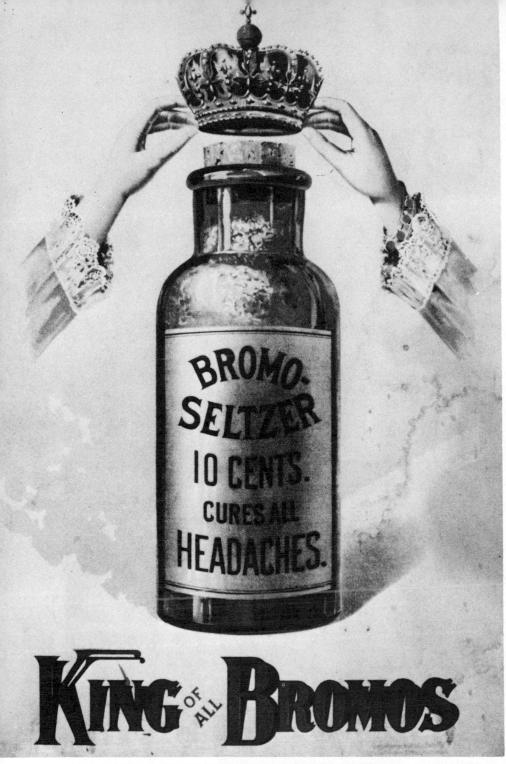

Bromo-Seltzer. Store poster. 24" × 36", c. 1900. Collection of Vivian and Ira Brichta.

Top: Pal Ade. Store sign, 24" × 28", c. 1940. Collection of Vivian and Ira Brichta. Bright children and a cute puppy have as wide an appeal today as they had in the 1940s. Bottom: Bromo-Seltzer. Store poster, 24" × 36", c. 1900. Collection of Vivian and Ira Brichta. One poster printed on both sides to influence the customer "coming and going."

Beech Nut Fruit Drops. Vending machine sign. c. 1930. Collection of Vivian and Ira Brichta.

Top: All Gone, NBC Graham Crackers. Poster, 16" × 20", c. 1920. Collection of Vivian and Ira Brichta. Bottom: Shell Oil. Billboard. c. 1930. Institute of Outdoor Advertising.

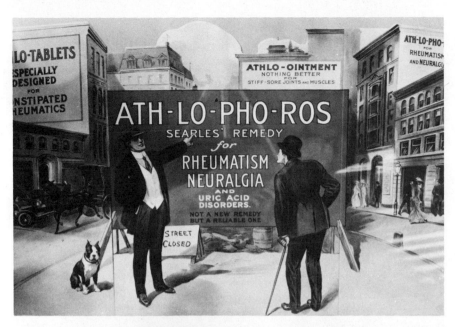

Styled for Youth

FORD V·8

Top: Ath-lo-pho-ros. Window sign, 18" × 22", c. 1915. Collection of Vivian and Ira Brichta. The street is closed to provide a perfect spot for an advertising sign. The artist, in his need to get the company's full line of products on one sign, used the sides of buildings for outdoor advertisements. Bottom: Ford. Billboard, c. 1939. Institute of Outdoor Advertising. In the depths of the Depression, Fords were selling for under $500. Right: Life Savers' Beechnut. C. 1920. Collection of Vivian and Ira Brichta. Edward Crane, an advertising salesman, bought a candy mint company in 1913 and packaged his mints in tin foil for saloons, barber shops, and drugstores. Crane's round mints competed with the free clover drops given away by saloonkeepers. When Crane placed a box of Life Savers next to store cash registers with a sign saying, "Take your change in Life Savers," store owners were soon collecting many nickels for packages sold.

Top five: Parmalee System Cabs. Handbills, c. 1927. Collection of Vivian and Ira Brichta. Bottom: Checker Taxi. Sign, 8" × 10", c. 1925. Collection of Vivian and Ira Brichta. The Checker Cab Manufacturing Company was founded in the early '20s by John Hertz of rent-a-car fame.

Paris Garters and Suspenders. Sign, c. 1930. Collection of Vivian and Ira Brichta. When garters gave way to stretch socks, and suspenders were abandoned for belts, A. Stein Company, manufacturer of Paris products, became one of the largest belt manufacturers in the country.

Top: W. B. Corsets. Billboard, c. 1929. Private collection. Left: $100,000 Collar Button. Store sign, 12″ × 14″, c. 1920. Collection of Vivian and Ira Brichta. The fact that this product was advertised in the popular Saturday Evening Post enhanced its credibility. Above: Royal Baking Company. Store sign, 28″ × 40″, c. 1930. Collection of Vivian and Ira Brichta. Courtesy of Standard Brands, Inc. Premiums, in this case a "beautiful Fairy Book," have been a successful merchandising ploy since the nineteenth century.

Above: Texas–Pacific. Billboard, c. 1935. Institute of Outdoor Advertising. The Indian with his peace-pipe was there to make sure the viewer remembered the company's initials. Right: Red Man Tobacco. Poster, 36" × 48", c. 1910. Collection of Vivian and Ira Brichta.

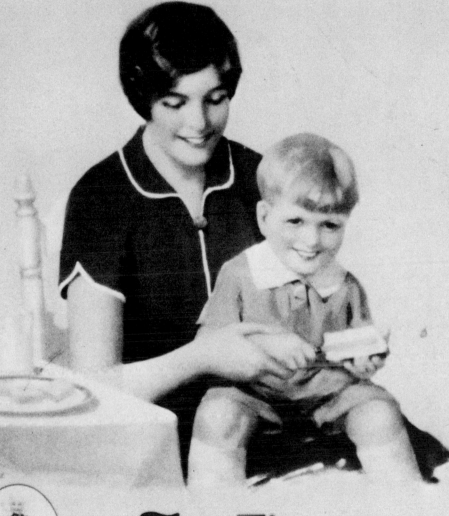

JELKE
GOOD LUCK
MARGARINE

National Biscuit Company. Advertising cards, 5" × 7", c. 1925. Collection of Vivian and Ira Brichta.

The Finest
Spread for Bread
Best for Cooking and Baking

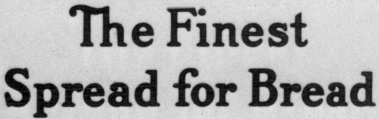

Jelkes' Good Luck Margarine. Sign, 14" × 18". c. 1930. Collection of Vivian and Ira Brichta. Courtesy of Lever Brothers Company. Before 1960, some states required that margarine be sold without artificial coloring. Margarine manufacturers packed yellow food coloring with their product and suggested that the user add the color. A few dairy states banned the sale of margarine entirely.

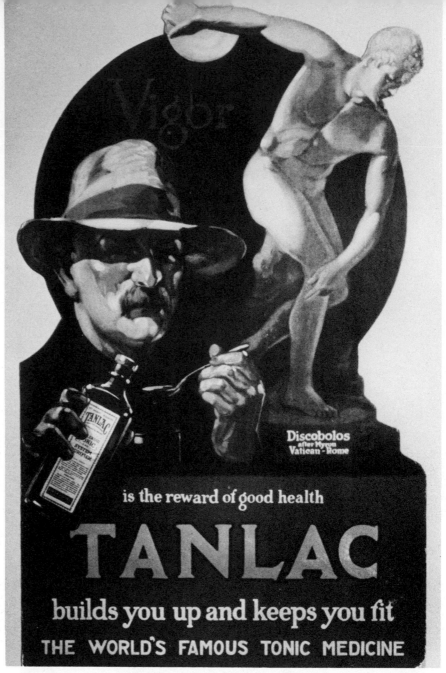

Discobolos
after Myron
Vatican - Rome

is the reward of good health

TANLAC

builds you up and keeps you fit
THE WORLD'S FAMOUS TONIC MEDICINE

Top: National Biscuit Company Graham Cracker. Poster, c. 1910. Collection of Vivian and Ira Brichta. Fifty years after this poster appeared, Wonder Bread was in litigation with the U.S. Government because of its claim, "Wonder Bread builds strong bodies 12 ways." Nabisco's statement that their crackers "make children sturdy" may have ended up in the same court if used today. Bottom: Toiletine. Mobile signs, c. 1915. Collection of Vivian and Ira Brichta.

Tanlac. Window sign, 12" × 15", c. 1927. Collection of Vivian and Ira Brichta. A shady character endorses Tanlac. Promoting patent medicines has been part of the American scene since the mid-1800s.

CHAPTER FOUR
LITTLE CARS AND BIG MACS:
1945-1976

The thirty years following World War II established a way of life as startlingly different from the prewar days as the 1930s were from the 1830s. While the advertising poster did not by itself play a key role in the changing life of America, it reflected the new lifestyles and fast maturing communications techniques of the postwar period.

The poster was still extensively used toward the end of the 1940s, but the technical explosions of the electronics industry and research into specialized fields such as demographics, psychographics, and marketing were to drastically change both the use and the look of advertising posters by 1960.

As the psychology of mass selling became a definable technique, the television industry, with its "slice-of-life" commercials—little dramas supposedly reflecting real-life situations—became the dominant force in the marketing of many products.

European economists who at the turn of the century had predicted that America would always be a land of millionaires continually gaining more millions as the working classes continued their futile uphill struggle were proved wrong by postwar realities. The war, along with a combination of tough income tax laws, labor union victories, and government subsidies and guarantees accomplished what congress and a major depression had failed to do: the country's wealth was redistributed through the strenghtening of the middle class.

Swift & Company. Outdoor "Spectacular," c. 1955. Foster & Kleiser. Courtesy of Swift and Company.

The wartime economy, which toward the mid-1940s ran with masterful efficiency and smoothness, remained in high gear right into the 1950's. With the lean years of the Depression and World War II behind them, Americans were learning to be consumers again.

Personal savings had increased substantially during the war, due in part to government controls on rents, wages, and prices. And since few items not essential to the war effort were being manufactured in those years, there was little opportunity to spend money on consumer goods. Government-sponsored advertising posters had advised Americans to put their earnings into war bonds in anticipation of the "good life" that was to be expected when the war ended. For most people, the acquisition of consumer goods was second in their dreams only to being reunited with a loved one fighting in Europe or in the Pacific.

Within a year or so after the war, upwards of ten million men and women were mustered out of the armed forces. Unlike the recession that followed World War I, however, the economy of the 1940s helped ease the readjustment to civilian life of many GI's.

Under the GI Bill of Rights, millions of Americans entered colleges and universities with financial assistance from the government. This caused immediate overcrowding of all existing facilities, and the ex-soldiers, frequently with wives and children, had to be housed in makeshift metal Quonset huts, which were hastily assembled by the besieged schools. The huts represented small improvement over the accommodations the veterans had known during the war, when wives followed husbands from training camp to training camp in remote areas of the United States. By 1950, over four million Bachelors degrees had been conferred on returning GI's.

The accelerated marriage rate of the war years was insignificant in comparison to the postwar marriage boom. This, in turn, led to a great increase in the birthrate, generating a market for goods and services that lasted for years.

The construction industry, in its rush to provide housing for the returned veterans and their families, built entire communities of housing developments that were generally ten to thirty miles from a city. In those days, energy was cheap and plentiful and builders were heedless of the costs of heat, light, cooling, and transportation to and from nearby cities. On the other hand, building materials were in short supply; the inferior lumber frequently used in these postwar constructions caused floors to buckle and roofs to tilt. Improper and inadequate sewage and plumbing facilities created problems for the new homeowners that were to intensify during the next decade. A popular song of that era

36. Fatima Cigarettes. Billboard. c. 1910. Collection of Vivian and Ira Brichta.
37. Ladyfair Swimwear. Store sign, 20" × 24", c. 1928. Collection of Vivian and Ira Brichta.
38. J. T. Plug Tobacco. Poster. c. 1905. Library of Congress.

was a lament about the "ticky-tacky" tract houses "all in a row" which were difficult to tell apart.

With one thousand dollars or less as a down payment, returning veterans were able to obtain convenient mortgage payment terms arranged by housing developers. Thousands of young families left the cities to raise their children on land of their own. The development suburbs, complete with schools, parks, playgrounds, and churches, opened a new way of life for the average family—a life that was free from the congestion and concrete of city streets.

For many people, consumer goods became visible symbols of financial success. Economists labeled this phenomenon "conspicuous consumption" or "America's upwardly mobile society," and manufacturers made the most of the prosperous days. Through technically improved products and brand-name advertising, marketing experts delineated specific, carefully defined images of what the "good life" should be. Air conditioners protruded from bedroom windows, automatic dishwashers and home laundry systems were taken as signs of successful living, particularly for those people who had lived through the Depression era as well as the war. Gas-powered lawn mowers were bought by homeowners with small suburban lawns, while swings and slides, concrete patios and barbecue pits competed for available space on postage-stamp-sized lots.

While the automobile, improvements in roads, and commuter transportation made it possible to live on the

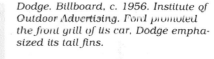

Dodge. Billboard. c. 1956. Institute of Outdoor Advertising. Ford promoted the front grill of its car. Dodge emphasized its tail fins.

outskirts of a city yet work in town, a second car in the family became a great convenience, since mother's responsibilities included shopping for the family and chauffeuring the children from sporting events to dancing classes through suburbs lacking in public transportation facilities. Conscious of the fact that a big "Olds" had more status than a Chevrolet, and the "four holer," a larger, more expensive Buick nicknamed for the four very prominent though nonfunctional holes on each side of the engine had more status than the smaller Buick "Special," which boasted only three holes, mother frequently chose the largest car the family could afford.

A second car in the family also helped spawn a new kind of selling arena, the shopping center. Clusters of dress shops, toy stores, drugstores, and supermarkets constructed close to high-density suburban areas shifted the focus still farther away from the cities and established the suburbs as self-contained communities. One by one, large department and chain stores opened suburban branches, accelerating a movement that had begun in the late 1920s, when Marshall Field & Company first opened stores in outlying areas of Chicago.

Once the transition from war to peace had begun, buying a brand-new fresh-smelling automobile topped the priority list of most Americans. After five years of keeping the old car going with retread tires and handmade spare parts, people were anxious to register with car dealers and buy an automobile as soon as one became available. Outdoor posters and signs in dealer showrooms advised potential customers to have patience until auto manufacturers could catch up with the demand for cars. General Motors, Ford, and Chrysler worked extra shifts to turn out millions of cars. By 1950, the auto industry was selling over eight million cars per year, more than had existed in the entire country following World War I.

In 1945, Henry J. Kaiser, the multimillionaire shipbuilder who had won national fame as an industrialist able to supply the armed forces with untold numbers of cargo-carrying ships, entered the automotive market. Kaiser applied his wartime expertise to producing automobiles and, within record time, was delivering cars to an eager market. But Ford, General Motors, and Chrysler had years of experience in styling, dealer service, sophisticated distribution systems, and carefully planned marketing programs, all of which proved too much for the newcomer. In an effort to save his floundering company, Kaiser produced a minicar called the Henry J. Priced around one-thousand dollars, the four-cylinder economy runabout used less gas than larger models. Unfortunately, it was a quarter of a century ahead of its time. Sears, Roebuck and Company tried to sell the Henry J in Chicago, but soon realized that Americans wanted the big cars they had dreamed of during the war years. Kaiser, however, went on to build real estate developments in Hawaii and, finally, to become head of one of the largest and most successful industrial companies in the world, the Kaiser Aluminum Company.

In the late 1940s, Raymond Loewy, the French-born industrial designer, made automotive history with his ultra-streamlined Studebaker, which some thought looked the same from both the front and the back. Ten years later, Studebaker, too, was forced to abandon its small share of the market.

34. Genuine Bull Durham. Store sign. 9″ × 12″, c. 1910. Collection of Vivian and Ira Brichta. Courtesy of American Brands, Inc. Reminiscent of a Renoir boating scene.

35. Famous Dukes. Store sign. 18″ × 24″, c. 1910. Collection of Vivian and Ira Brichta. Courtesy of American Brands, Inc. In 1910, the Duke family owned 82 percent of all the tobacco business in the United States. The "Famous Dukes" poster was one of a series using these dapper midgets as models.

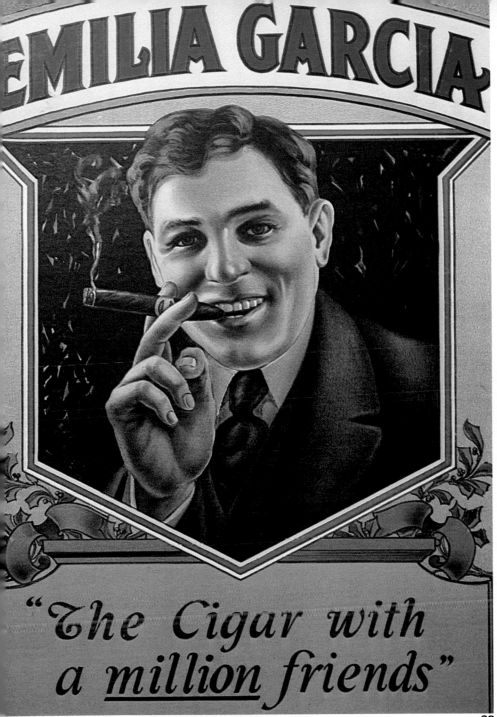

EMILIA GARCIA

"The Cigar with a <u>million</u> friends"

39

Colonial Club CIGAR

41

Give me fish that *bite*

and tobacco that DON'T!

GRANGER ROUGH CUT

40

43. Christian Diehl Brewing Company. Poster, 18″ × 24″, c. 1920. Collection of Vivian and Ira Brichta.
44. Butter Nut Bread. Sign, 8″ × 10″, c. 1930. Collection of Vivian and Ira Brichta. Interstate Brands Corporation, bakers of Butter Nut Bread and Dolly Madison Cakes.
45. Munsingwear. Poster, 28″ × 40″, c. 1930. Collection of Vivian and Ira Brichta. A 1930s example of the slender, long-legged look, typically associated with the American Girl.

2. William Kemp Brewing Company. ster, c. 1916. Library of Congress. nis poster might have been inspired by Dutch portrait.

Hitch your *writing* to a star

Parker Duofold

46

"Ideal"
Waterman

48

Because we like
POST'S BRAN FLAKES
we eat it every day

Post's
BRAN
FLAKES
WHEAT

47

Imperial.
The Cream of All Ice Creams.

49

46. Parker Pen. Poster, 28″ × 35″, c. 1927. Collection of Vivian and Ira Brichta. When Lindbergh became the world's hero by flying non-stop from New York to Paris, his plane, *The Spirit of St. Louis,* was celebrated as well. Parker suggests "you hitch your writing to a star."

47. Post's Bran. Store poster, 16″ × 30″, c. 1930. Collection of Vivian and Ira Brichta. Post's is a registered trademark of General Foods Corporation. Subliminally, the poster asks, "Wouldn't you like your family to look as healthy and happy as this one?"

48. Waterman's Pen. Poster, c. 1920. Library of Congress. A French approach by Jean d'Ylen.

49. Imperial Ice Cream. Poster, 15″ × 30″, c. 1928. Collection of Vivian and Ira Brichta. The girls of the Roaring Twenties enjoyed bathtub gin, short skirts, jazz, and ice cream!

50. Waterman's Ideal Fountain Pen. Poster, 30″ × 40″, c. 1910. Collection of Vivian and Ira Brichta. At the end of the nineteenth century the C. E. Waterman Company held contests with church groups and other social organizations to find slogans usable in their ads. They paid $25.00 for slogans to be considered and $1,000 to the winners.

Waterman's
Ideal
Fountain Pen
Saves
the dip
"Well, I'll be durned!"

The first wheat food
with a real-
hustle-down-
to-breakfast-
taste

Kellogg's
Krumbles
TRADE MARK

LLOYD J. HARRISS *Pies*

52

54

52. Lloyd J. Harriss Pies. Poster, c. 1920. Library of Congress. George Washington crossed the Delaware amidst a mass of cherry pie.

53. Kellogg's Corn Flakes. Poster, c. 1920. Library of Congress. Reprinted with permission of Kellogg Company.

54. Kellogg's Pep. Poster, c. 1920. Library of Congress. Reprinted with permission of Kellogg Company. An endorsement from The Boy Scouts of America created an effective poster.

55. Sinclair H-C Gasoline. Poster, 24" × 36", c. 1933. Collection of Vivian and Ira Brichta. A strong graphic image illustrating the many cars on the road during the '30s. H-C Sinclair is one of the long-gone gasoline brands of that time.

55

53

51. Kellogg's Krumbles. Window sign, 5" × 30", c. 1920. Collection of Vivian and Ira Brichta. Reprinted with permission of Kellogg Company.

56. Merita Bread. Embossed lithograph on metal, 22″ × 28″, c. 1939. Collection of Vivian and Ira Brichta. Visual tie-in for popular radio program during the late 1930s and 1940s.

56

59

59. Wrigley's Gum. Streetcar card, c. 1942. Collection of Vivian and Ira Brichta. Reprinted with permission of William Wrigley, Jr., Company.

57

57, 58. Lux. Posters, c. 1930. Collection of Vivian and Ira Brichta. These posters show a strong Art Deco influence.

58

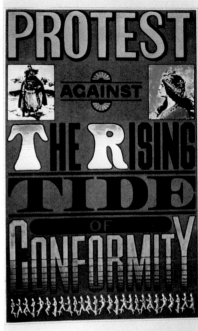

64

60. 7-Up. Billboard, c. 1970. The 7-Up Company.
61. 7-Up. Billboard, c. 1970. The 7-Up Company.
62. 7-Up. Billboard, c. 1970. The 7-Up Company.
63. B. F. Goodrich Company. Store poster, 35″ × 45″, c. 1975. Courtesy of B. F. Goodrich Company. The age of the "smart ad," originated by Volkswagen, Levi's, and Levy's Rye Bread extended into every office on Madison Avenue. Humor coupled with illustrations was "in" and became the trademark of some of America's most able poster artists.
64. Booth's House of Lords. Poster, c. 1967. Private collection.

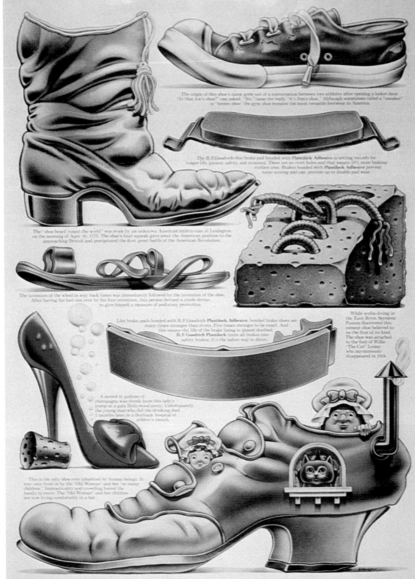

63

Refreshing

Coca-Cola
REG. U.S. PAT. OFF.

Fly the new Honda XL-250.

This rider is a professional. Honda recommends that you riders not attempt difficult stunts. ©1972 American Honda Motor Co., Inc.

65. Coca-Cola. Billboard, c. 1950. Courtesy of Coca-Cola Company. This 1950s outdoor 24-sheet billboard poster displays the style, warmth, and good taste associated with Coke's advertising over the last 75 years. Coca-Cola is a registered trademark of the Coca-Cola Company.

Tan Hawaiian **TANYA**
COCONUT OIL
AND COCOA BUTTER

66. Honda. Billboard, c. 1970. Institute of Outdoor Advertising.
67. Tanya. Billboard, c. 1970. Institute of Outdoor Advertising.

Is nothing sacred?

68

69

68. Volkswagen. Billboard, c. 1965–1970. Institute of Outdoor Advertising.
69. Black Velvet. Billboard, c. 1970. Institute of Outdoor Advertising. The double entendre used in advertising.
70. Volkswagen. Billboard, c. 1965–1970. Institute of Outdoor Advertising.

70

Family Plan.

Le Sabre by BUICK

71

Wing it

1976 Buick Skyhawk

72

71. Buick. Billboard. c. 1977. McCann-
Erickson Company.
72. Buick. Billboard. c. 1976. McCann-
Erickson Company.

73. Levi's Jeans. Store poster, 1970s. Courtesy of Levi Strauss & Company.
74. Levi's Jeans. Store poster, 1970s. Courtesy of Levi Strauss & Company.
75. Levi's Jeans. Store poster, 1970s. Courtesy of Levi Strauss & Company.

76. (Overleaf) Levi's Jeans. Store poster, 1970s. Courtesy of Levi Strauss & Company.

McDonald's. Billboard, c. 1977. Mc-Donald's® Inc.

comfortable bathrooms, and serve reasonably priced meals and ice creams in many flavors. Howard Johnson pioneered his carefully regulated fast food franchise in the 1930s. He sold permission to operate as well as instructions on doing business to individuals willing to pay for the Howard Johnson know-how, advertising support, and image.

During the 1950s, Colonel Sanders became the king of Southern fried chicken. In that same decade, Ray Kroc, a malted-milk mixer salesman, purchased a hamburger stand in California from the McDonald brothers. Within a few years Kroc parlayed his purchase into a string of standardized "golden arch" hamburger stands operating all across the country. It was also in the fifties that Kemmons Wilson built a motel outside of Memphis, Tennessee, and called it Holiday Inn. Its success heralded the vast motel chains to come.

In 1958, the economist John Kenneth Galbraith published *The Affluent Society*, a book that acknowledged America's economic coming of age and stated that the challenge facing the country would be coming to terms with its great abundance rather than with scarcity. During the years that factories had turned out huge quantities of consumer goods, advertising had played a vital part in defining and enchancing America as a society of consumers.

By the end of World War II there were about thirty-two hundred advertising agencies in the United States, and in 1960 this number had increased to fifty-five hundred. Until the 1960s, the primary responsibility of the advertising agency was to write and design ads and to place those ads where most people could see or hear them. The skyscraper buildings along New York's Madison Avenue and Chicago's Michigan Avenue housed many big advertising agencies, which were expert in promoting products through radio commercials, and billboard, magazine, and newspaper advertising. Before television, radio was considered to be the prime advertising media. Advertising people wrote jingles and negotiated with network and publication sales representatives for the purchase of broadcast time and magazine space.

In an effort to keep pace with their clients' new products and brand names, advertising agencies developed more and more specialized departments. Each department was organized to help move goods efficiently and smoothly through various channels of distribution and, ultimately, on to the consumer. Art directors and copywriters formed creative teams to work with college-trained specialists in sales promotion, marketing, and public relations. They developed advertising messages that appealed to both their client and his customers. Highly skilled research personnel investigated the public's reaction to a product even before it was for sale in the stores. Research techniques became so finely tuned to public preferences in colors, shapes, sizes, and prices that the thoughts and feelings of prospective buyers could, to a large extent, be reported for any area of the country, be it rural or urban. Special research firms such as A. C. Nielson and Company (best known for its broadcast surveys) and Market Facts, Inc. also added to advertising agency knowledge by measuring public reaction to products ranging from cereals to cosmetics.

The greatest era for manufacturers as well as for advertising agencies started in the 1950s with the mass production of television sets and regularly scheduled television programming. Television helped make mass marketing a reality. Never before had so potent an information, education, and entertainment medium been made available to the general public for such a small price. Ten percent down and small payments each month could bring that seven-inch picture tube into anyone's home. No invention with the speed and impact of the televised picture had ever before reached human beings.

Marlboro Shirts. Poster, c. 1946. Private collection. One of the few American posters by designer Lucian Bernhard.

Though the telephone had been invented nearly half a century earlier, years and years were to pass before most American homes had telephones. The automobile, too, remained more of a curiosity than a widespread mode of transportation in its early years. But television hit the American market like a lightning bolt, and, in less than ten years, 60 percent of all American homes had sets.

In the earliest days of the medium, television programs were "live" and broadcast was limited to evening hours. Frequently the sponsors were actually present in the studios making suggestions as the show and its commerials progressed. New owners were so enthralled to have television sets in their homes that they often watched station test patterns. By the latter part of the 1950s, most shows were filmed or taped prior to broadcast.

Quiz shows, like Revlon's "The $64,000 Question" and Stopette spray deodorant's "What's My Line?" captured prime-time adult audiences. General Foods, Mattel, and Kellogg introduced their new products via Saturday morning cartoon shows directed to children. Psychologists discussed the merits and disadvantages of watching television to the exclusion of family interaction and predicted dire problems for children allowed to watch whenever they wished.

Even with stars like Elvis Presley, the dominance of the motion picture industry as an entertainment medium was threatened by television. With television providing free movies, sporting events, and dramas to thirty-six million viewers every day, the movie playing at the local theater had to be exceptional to lure people away from their living-room television sets.

By 1965, five thousand motion picture theaters had gone out of business; most of the companies that produced motion pictures had been purchased by conglomerates and were producing television material as well as movies.

Like the movies, radio broadcasting wavered in importance during the early years of television. Once directed exclusively to mother during the so-called housewife hours, the period between 10:00 A.M. and 3:00 P.M., radio lost its appeal as more and more hours of programming were scheduled by television stations. However, the radio industry was revitalized by the rock-oriented teen market and the sophisticated new designs in portable radios. The Beatles and other early rock stars created an audience of young listeners who kept radio alive. In 1955, the first year Elvis Presley was under contract to RCA, he sold ten million records and half again as many posters. In the early sixties, the Beatles eclipsed Presley and every other performer of their time, selling records, posters, and other tie-in merchandise in astronomical quantities.

With thousands of products being manufactured or imported into the country daily, only the nation's top one hundred corporations, responsible for approximately 55 percent of all advertising, could afford to buy advertising on prime-time television shows. Most advertisers still used newspapers, magazines, store posters, billboards, and local broadcasting to keep their products before the public. The retail industry, including stores that sold television sets, was among the last to use television advertising.

Key to the growth in the sales of television sets was installment buying. Although it had been instituted in the eighteenth century by the clock salesman Eli Terry and although both Ford and General Motors had offered automobiles on time-payment plans during the 1920s, "buying on time" did not become widespread until the late 1940s. With a few dollars down, deep freezers, dining-room furniture, and other expensive items could be sent home immediately and paid for slowly with a few dollars each month. The "buy now, pay later" attitude loosened the inhibitions of many people and helped enlarge the market for such luxuries as motorboats, trailers, motorbikes, and even European vacations.

Department stores, gasoline companies, and restaurants showed Americans another way to make purchases without having cash in hand. It was the credit card, the logical next step beyond installment buying. Credit cards allowed people to buy on impulse, and "charging it" became an accepted way to shop. Credit cards gave the illusion that high living was accessible to everyone, and often the utmost discipline was needed not to exceed one's financial capacity.

By the middle 1960s, material consumption as a way

of life was being rejected by many of the post-World War II youth who had grown to young adulthood. They could not accept their parents' continual striving for affluence and the status that went with it. Young people found no evidence that affluence brought happiness. Within the counterculture of the late 1960s was a rejection of technology that signaled an implicit denial of material values. The complex social order wrought by their elders seemed undesirable to many young Americans who thought their road to happiness lay in simplifying their lives. Unwilling to become part of their parents' world, youngsters left home, walking and hitchhiking their way across the country, or became "flower children" able to identify with only a growing drug culture. Others moved to rural communes and lived under primitive conditions.

Although young middle-class Americans were beginning to rebel against the consumer culture by the mid-sixties, when Lyndon Johnson gave his State of the Union address in January 1964, one-fifth of the nation was still living below the poverty level. Johnson declared "unconditional war on poverty" and proclaimed the beginning of a Great Society, which represented the democratic ideal that all Americans should and could enjoy the highest standard of living in the world.

America's military commitment in Vietnam stimulated the economy to some degree, but unlike wars that preceded it the Vietnam conflict was resisted by a large segment of the public, who ultimately helped bring it to a halt.

The sit-ins, protest marches and demonstrations that helped end the Vietnam war were also used to raise the consciousness of white Americans in an effort to assure civil rights for black people. The attitudes of change toward blacks during the 1960s resulted in important differences in how they were portrayed in advertisements. Around the time of the Civil War, posters had been designed to appeal to whites, and blacks were usually portrayed in a derogatory manner. In the 1880s, the image of the black began to change as the social value of railroad porters, chefs, and nursemaids was acknowledged. Rastus and Aunt Jemima, two black trademark figures, served their white employers cheerfully. In the 1930s, Amos n' Andy, played by white actors Freeman Gosden and Charles Correll, were among America's most popular radio characters. The fact that they were only a notch or two above the old minstrel show stereotypes did not impede anyone's enjoyment of their earthy humor.

As continual refinements in market research resulted in segmentation by ethnic groups, blacks were recognized as a distinct consumer class and advertising began to be directed specifically to them. Such segmentation occurred with greater frequency during the 1950s and 1960s as magazines like *Jet* and *Ebony* sold black-oriented products and black-oriented commercials ran in movie houses in black neighborhoods. During the 1970s, posters and billboards reflected the improving economic and social status of blacks and showed them enjoying life in luxurious settings.

As the image of black people evolved in advertisements from that of servants to fully privileged citizens, stereotypes of women, too, changed in the minds of advertisers. Before World War I, poster advertisements were aimed at men, who generally allocated the family's income. Posters selling beer and tobacco featured decorative women with hourglass figures. By the early 1920s, as they began to do more and more of the family's shopping, women were used as models for clothing, cars, and cough medicines. Advertisers believed that women responded to other women: The Palmolive girl of the 1930s echoed women's newly won rights to vote and work, while the cheesecake models of World War II relied on kittenlike sex appeal to sell their advertisers' products. Many advertisers believed that a sexually desirable woman is a potent sales tool. They feel that her form and face embodies the dreams of a desirable life for many people. Charles Revson's idea of sensuous women continually primping themselves for the approval of others is clearly reflected by his Revlon girls of the 1950s and 1960s. The Revlon models, personally chosen by Revson, have proven a powerful stimulus to the sale of cosmetics. Although more and more advertisements show women in positions of authority, advertisers still depend on the sex appeal of women. But, even if the stereotype of females as sex objects is still with us, the physical image of women has changed over the years. Psyche, the lovely White Rock beverage symbol, who had gone topless until recently, has in eighty years grown four inches taller and lost twenty-two pounds!

During the late 1940s, many of the women who had worked during World War II relinquished their jobs to returning veterans. Like the soldiers they had replaced on the job, women felt the war years had interrupted their lives. While they were pleased to have helped their country and to have earned money during this time, many of them were anxious to go back to the task of being wives and mothers. In the 1960s, however, the women's liberation movement, which preached equality of the sexes, particularly in the labor market, coupled with an expanding inflationary economy, gave women the impetus to seek employment once again. Women challenged all-male universities to open their doors, and many entered business and the professions—not for a few years until babies were born, but as lifetime careers. Some who went to work did

White Rock. Metal sign, c. 1930. Collection of Vivian and Ira Brichta. The winged, fairylike creature who served as the White Rock trademark went through phases of being covered and uncovered, depending on the morals of the time.

so to provide essentials for themselves and their children in a time when divorce and marriage rates were nearly equal. Others worked to augment their husbands' salaries. Frequently, a second income broadened a family's purchasing power and created additional markets for better homes, expensive clothing, and college educations for their children.

Advertising was one of the first professions to open its doors to women. Agency policymakers believed that women could sell to other women. Although female copywriters, creative directors, and account executives responsible for television advertising abounded in many advertising agencies, television still featured commercials showing women rapturously exclaiming over a toilet tissue that "squishes" as it is squeezed or screaming with delight upon discovering bargain floor mops. Women of the 1970s who compete in a working world, however, are reevaluating such commercials. More and more they purchase a product, particularly one sold in grocery stores, in terms of its utilitarian service. They want value for the dollars they spend. Women are responsible for the trend toward generic labeling of both drugs and foods. A sack of name-brand flour or sugar costs more than similar items labeled simply "flour" or "sugar," while generally providing the same quality.

During the 1960s, an onslaught of media prodded, urged, tempted, and reminded the public of products and services that could make their lives more fun, more rewarding, or easier. Americans responded by buying and rebuying goods they already owned since many products were built to wear out, break, or go out of fashion. Built-in obsolescence was the order of the day. Manufacturers and advertising agencies had made America style conscious. Without major retooling, automotive manufacturers could produce new model cars each year, changed from the previous year's model only cosmetically. Fashionable refrigerators were first made to defrost themselves, then made in gold or green with two doors instead of one, and finally fitted with automatic icemakers. Soon scrap heaps of rusted automobiles and discarded refrigerators and washing machines ringed the cities. Garbage littered the nation as automobile riders filled the countryside with empty beverage cans and wrappings from fast-food restaurant fare. The unsightly junkyards prompted the Johnson administration to pass the Highway Beautification Act in the hope that "visual pollution" could be eliminated. Ecologists publicized the glut of yesterday's goods in their attempt to preserve America's natural beauty.

New magazines as well as new television shows appeared and disappeared with amazing swiftness in the 1960s and 1970s. Mass circulation periodicals such as the *Saturday Evening Post, Look,* and *Life* had been abandoned by a public who preferred television to magazines, although all of those magazines are again being published today. As readership dwindled, advertisers no longer found many of the mass-oriented publications useful. Cyrus K. Curtis, once publisher of the *Ladies Home Journal*, told a group of business executives that his magazine was published not to benefit the American woman, but to give manufacturers a chance to sell women their products. In 1977, the Chicago *Daily News*, the last of Chicago's evening papers, followed many other urban newspapers and ceased publication, primarily because advertisers found other media, notably television, more suitable to the needs of their products and more compatible with the frequently fickle tastes of a public who preferred televised evening news, weather, and sports to the printed word.

The popular magazines today are edited for clearly defined but limited markets. They are more expensive than were most mass-directed publications and are tailor-made for equipment and specialty manufacturers to advertise in them. Generally, these periodicals reflect current trends and lifestyles. Some of the most successful relate to skiing, running, antique collecting, and gourmet cooking.

Because televised commercials became so familiar to Americans, print advertising has changed over the last twenty years. Foods, liquors, furniture, and fashions are now more often photographed than drawn. Like their televised counterparts, true-to-life people, are more popular than professional models as spokesmen these days. Dramatic close-up camera shots of foods fill magazine ads with rich, warm colors and tempt their readers to taste the moistness of a Betty Crocker cake or to feel the smoothness of a slice of Kraft cheese. Realistic photographs have almost completely replaced the illustrations of food packages that had been used in print advertising until the end of World War II.

In the world of fashion, where a design can become dated within weeks after it leaves the drawing board, the use of contemporary photography helps the industry maintain a "you-need-it-now" image for the career-minded woman with little time to shop. Contemporary photography also captures the mood automotive manufactures want for their product, whether that mood is romanticism, low-cost practicality, Volkswagen whimsy, or Cadillac wealth. Since automobiles became status symbols, manufacturers have carefully identified each of many special markets. Cars are photographed on the edge of lofty cliffs, on beaches with dogs and children, in the middle of airports, and with sleek leopards and sleeker women. Advertising, with its appeal to human emotions, remains the vital link between the automaker and the car fantasies of his public.

Swift's Premium. Billboard, c. 1960. Institute of Outdoor Advertising. Courtesy of Swift and Company.

The dream cars of the 1970s and 1980s would surprise Alfred Sloan, who built General Motors on the premise that Americans would always want larger and more stylish automobiles. When Volkswagens were first imported from Germany, people dubbed the stubby-looking little car the "beetle." An imaginative advertising campaign made a virtue of the Volkswagen's small size and lack of style. Print ads and billboards emphasized its positive values of low gas consumption and minimal emission of pollutants. Because the Volkswagen style rarely changed, advertising played up the fact that damaged or worn parts could be replaced with those of a later year. Created by the New York agency of Doyle, Dane Bernbach, Volkswagen's ads were witty, understated, and entertaining. Their humor flew in the face of early copywriter Claude Hopkins' dictum that people wouldn't buy from clowns. The appeal to a new consumer attitude was epitomized by one of Volkswagen's slogans: "Think small." When motorcycles became popular in the early seventies, Kawasaki did Volkswagen one better with a billboard showing a Kawasaki cycle in front of a VW beetle with the slogan "Think even smaller."

The Volkswagen had a great appeal for young people. Exposure to television of the 1960s and 1970s had given them an economic sophistication that few of their parents had had at their age. The young became tastemakers rather

Volkswagen. Billboard, c. 1965. Private collection. Volkswagen was advertised as an inexpensive second car.

Kawasaki Motorcycle. Billboard, c. 1972. Private collection.

than followers of their elders, and their power as consumers was recognized by advertisers. Not only were they major purchasers of small cars, but they also bought records, clothing, stereo systems, and related electronic products.

Just as the Volkswagen campaign was targeted to specific segments of the population, so were many other ad campaigns. In fact, by the 1970s such targeting had become a common way to advertise. Products so advertised were said to have "brand image." The Marlboro man with his rugged individualism was meant to appeal to the *macho* male, although Marlboro cigarettes had originally been developed for women. Virginia Slims were aimed at the self-sufficient, style-conscious woman. Designating a particular way to use a product—Ny-Quil, the "night-time cold remedy," and Correctol, "the woman's gentle laxative"—and directing advertisements of that product to a specific group of people was labeled "positioning" by advertising agencies.

In the early 1970s, cigarette commercials were banned from television. Tobacco manufacturers moved their advertising from broadcast media to print, using magazine ads, outdoor posters, and signs on the sides of city buses to tell their story to the public.

Although posters no longer are the prime advertising media of the 1970s and 1980s, they act to reinforce televised commercials and other advertisements. Merrill Lynch, the brokerage firm, uses handsomely framed posters in each of its offices to remind visitors that "Merrill Lynch is bullish on America," an echo of their well-established television theme. In addition, posters frequently serve to bolster corporate images by keeping the public aware of the good name and charitable deeds of various corporations.

When posters are used today as advertising media, great emphasis is placed on their art and design. Teams of copywriters, artists, and creative directors are responsible for integrating well-designed graphics with provocative phrases in order to stimulate sales.

A great influx of European artists before and during World War II brought such men as Herbert Bayer, Lazlo Moholy-Nagy, Joseph Albers, and Herbert Matter to America. They had a major influence on American advertising graphics through their own work and through the training of other designers. In the 1950s, Saul Bass, Paul Rand, and others created posters that reflected international design trends, and a large number of manufacturers recognized their value. Many of these posters announced films and art exhibits, but product advertising was definitely influenced by their innovations.

Otis Shepard, who produced billboards for the Wrigley Company, was one of the first designers to use a European style of simplified drawing. Shepard's billboards for Wrigley's gum were in the vanguard of American advertising art for many years. William Wrigley, the company's founder, always wanted more copy and less art, but Shepard insisted that the picture be dominant.

The visual philosophy that "less is more" began in the 1960s with minimalist art. The minimalists believed in reducing an image to its ultimate limit. Squares, rectangles, and circles of plastic and chromium decorated art museums and public parks. Like the abstract expressionists before them who had frequently painted enormous canvases, minimalists understood that in order to attract and hold the public's attention their work had to be of considerable size. Poster artists also realized that they were competing

Merrill Lynch. Poster, c. 1976. Merrill Lynch.

for attention with hundreds and hundreds of visual messages received daily by the average American as he moved swiftly from job to home to store. The proposition that "less is more" suited a media-saturated society able to travel fast and far. Soon billboards with only one or two words of copy and instantly comprehensible large, clear pictures with but a few details appeared in the cities and along the country's highways.

Volkswagen, Levy's rye bread, 7-Up, and the Levi Strauss Company are a few of the manufacturers who successfully used the minimalist approach. The Levi Strauss campaigns are geared to youth. The company started in San Francisco during the Gold Rush, selling heavy-duty workpants to miners, cowboys, and stagecoach drivers. Levi Strauss continued to produce men's work clothes until young people of both sexes discovered their usefulness and made them the uniform of youth-conscious America and, currently, of the whole world.

In the 1960s, Levy's Rye Bread, which was sold locally in New York, achieved national fame with an advertising campaign that used ethnicity with tongue in cheek. A series of posters appeared in subway stations throughout the city, each featuring a photograph of an ethnic type—an Italian mother, a black child, an Irish choirboy—with the slogan, "You don't have to be Jewish to love Levy's real Jewish rye." The campaign's acknowledgment of America's ethnic amalgam was a success in New York, where people of different ethnic groups had been living side by side for years. Levy's advertising was an early example of brash copy derived from street humor carefully calculated to reach a special audience.

On the other hand, Levi Strauss posters were frequently not used out-of-doors at all but were hung in stores that carried the company's merchandise. Among the artists who created the Levi image are Bruce Wolfe, Victor Moscoso, a leading underground comic and rock

Levi's Jeans. Store Poster, c. 1970. Courtesy of Levi Strauss & Company.

CHEWING GUM

"Wrigley's" is a name most Americans readily identify as a brand of chewing gum. Through innovative packaging, advertising, and selling, the company has made gum so popular that it sells an average of 175 sticks of gum per year to every American.

Wrigley was not the first company to make gum. The Adams family of Boston had made a chewable chicle-based product fifty years before Wrigley came on the scene. The Adams product, Black Jack gum, is still available today. Beeman's pepsin-flavored gum is another old-timer that has been sold in drug and candy stores for decades. But the Beeman's slogan, "Helps you eat like a pig," was a desirable pitch in pre-Victorian days.

Originally gum was made from chicle, a substance that comes from a plant grown in Mexico, the Amazon Valley, and the South Pacific islands. During World War II, Japanese submarines cut off America's supply of chicle and manufacturers turned to a synthetic product called polyvinyl acetate, which is still used today.

Otis Shepard's art-deco, wholesome looking Doublemint Twins were familiar sights to millions of subway, bus, streetcar, and commuter train passengers.

Wrigley posters, advertised on public transport for the past fifty years, have kept the Wrigley image of clean, healthy living fresh in the public mind.

Wrigley's Gum. Streetcar card, c. 1930. Reprinted with permission of William Wrigley, Jr. Company. Otis Shepard's Art Deco illustrations were familiar to streetcar and subway riders for over 25 years.

poster artist during the Haight-Ashbury days, and Charles White III and Dave Willardson, who are known for their airbrush illustrations on record album covers.

The 7-Up campaigns also drew on new imagery, but with more caution. "Wet and Wild" was the original theme, but researchers found that many people identified soft drinks with cola. Milton Glaser, Barry Zaid, and other designers seldom previously invited to work on product advertising created billboards proclaiming 7-Up as an alternative to cola drinks, the "Uncola."

Late in the 1960s, Ralph Nader, a young lawyer working in Washington, DC, wrote a book that was to change the course of advertising significantly. Entitled *Unsafe at Any Speed*, the book was an indictment of General Motors for misleading advertising and for the manufacture and marketing of its compact car, the Corvair. Nader contended that General Motors knew the Corvair to be unsafe, yet chose to ignore that fact and continued to manufacture and promote it. Nader appeared as a youthful David attacking the Goliath of General Motors as he took unprecedented legal action to stop GM from making fraudulent claims for the Corvair. General Motors countered by hiring detectives to investigate Nader, hoping to discredit him professionally.

Nader won his case against GM, and he became the father of a new consumer movement to protect the public against devious product claims. The press labeled Ralph Nader and his group of young, enthusiastic workers "Nader's Raiders." The Raiders called attention to many consumer problems and moved the Federal Trade Commission to end some of the more flagrantly misleading advertisements.

By 1970, "truth in advertising" had become the byword of the advertising business, and advertising agency legal departments scrutinized every ad. The FTC sued the Continental Baking Company for stating that its product, Wonder Bread, "Built Strong Bodies 12 Ways," a slogan that seemed to suggest that similar breads were nutritionally inferior. The FTC won its case against Continental and then took legal steps to stop Warner Lambert, the drug manufacturer, from claiming that its mouthwash, Listerine, cured colds or sore throats.

Promise- and product-watching has become a recognized profession. Watchers like Betty Furness and Bess Myerson have earned the respect of manufacturers and consumers alike, and publications reporting on the reliability of foods, drugs, and other products proliferate.

In 1980, American advertising will be a 50-billion-dollar-plus business, a most formidable industry. Advertising, mindful of its ability to sell products and services, also helps

7-Up Company. Billboard, c. 1965–1975. The 7-Up Company.

7-Up Company. Billboard, c. 1965–1975. The 7-Up Company.

sell causes. Under the auspices of the Advertising Council, volunteer professionals create campaigns to encourage the fight against cancer and to discourage the use of tobacco. Smokey the Bear has long been one of the Council's most able spokesmen.

As the 1980s begin, the computer has become indispensible and color television sets and home video recorders, which allow viewers to record and play back television programs, are accessible to increasing numbers of Americans. Cable television has already made available at least thirty channels, permitting broadcasters to cater to special segments of the population much as current magazines do. The communications technology of home computers and international satellite broadcasting promises a revolution in information gathering and dissemination greater than any known before.

A decade ago, Americans were fast approaching a state of information overload when Alvin Toffler introduced the term "future shock" to denote an individual's state of mind as the rate of change exceeded his ability to adapt to it. "New discoveries, new technologies, new social arrangements in the external world," said Toffler, "erupt into our lives in the form of increased turnover rates—shorter and shorter relational durations. They force a faster and faster pace of daily life. They demand new levels of adaptability."

The rate of technological innovation in the late 1970s increased swiftly and products changed virtually overnight. Manufacturers who were leaders in their fields a few years ago have yielded to other more inventive, more aggressive, or more marketing-oriented companies. Although predicted problems with energy might well change tomorrow's technological advancements, on the horizon are still greater changes, such as designs for enormous outdoor holograms which project three-dimensional product images into space. In a hundred years, the poster and the billboard may be considered quaint cultural artifacts. Meanwhile, they are still a part of our environment, continuing to shape the tastes and visual vocabulary of modern man.

THE AUTOMOBILE

The automobile is responsible for more social and economic changes in the United States than any other manufactured product. In 1925, there were 17.5 million cars in America and a Model T Ford cost two hundred and ninety dollars. Our national love affair with the automobile heightened during World War II when new cars were unavailable. The intense postwar desire to buy cars and the close relationship between the well-being of our nation's economy and the financial health of the automobile manufacturers reinforced the slogan, "As General Motors goes, so goes the nation."

During the early 1950s, automobile ownership, based on easy monthly payment plans, allowed Americans to move out of the cities. Suburbs were carved out of cornfields and carpooling of children along with drop-off-pick-up-kiss-and-run commuting husbands became a way of life. Conversely, cars enabled factories, once jammed together in inner cities, to move into the country where they could expand less expensively, yet be easily accessible to their employees.

By the mid 1970s, there were one hundred million cars on the road, one for every two Americans. Four out of five people drove to work, and car owners were spending more than fifty billion dollars per year for gas and oil, and over thirty billion dollars for auto maintenance.

In addition to consuming vast amounts of precious fuel, automobiles were responsible for other significant problems, not the least of which were air pollution in major metropolitan areas and a tremendous number of traffic accidents.

Chevrolet. Billboard, c. 1957. Foster & Kleiser, Chicago.
Chevrolet. Billboard, c. 1960. Foster & Kleiser.
Chevrolet. Billboard, c. 1960. Institute of Outdoor Advertising.

Pontiac. Billboard, c. 1976. Foster & Kleiser, Los Angeles.

Mother's little helper.

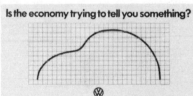

Volkswagen. Billboard, c. 1965–1970. Private collection.

Top: Volkswagen. Billboard, c. 1965–1970. Private collection. Center: Ford. Billboard, c. 1956. Institute of Outdoor Advertising. Bottom: Plymouth. Painted sign, c. 1969. Foster & Kleiser.

135

PACKAGING

Andreas Bernhardt, a sixteenth-century English papermaker, wrapped his product in packages and stamped his insignia on each one—thus was product packaging born.

Before supermarkets became popular, food packages were fairly utilitarian; they were used primarily to enclose and protect the contents of the package. Once the shopper was left along to stroll down the aisles of self-service markets, however, packages became product salesmen. Wrappings and boxes with bold colors, large type, and creative designs competed with one another on every shelf.

Today, motivation and research experts keep manufacturers up to date not only on the designs most likely to appeal to customers, but also on the size and shape of packages convenient for use. Frequently, photographs of the product temptingly arranged on its package have enticed shoppers who automatically relate the printed picture to the televised commercials familiar to them.

Truth in Packaging, the government-sponsored program started in the 1970s, has changed the concept of what a package ought to do for its product. In addition to protection of contents, convenience in size and shape, and attractive design, a package now offers valuable information on how best to use the product and lists the specific ingredients and nutritional values to be found therein.

Jack in the Box. Billboard, c. 1971. Private collection. Courtesy of Jack in the Box Restaurant Division, Foodmaker, Inc.

Top: McDonald's. Store poster, c. 1975. McDonald's® Inc. Bottom: Budweiser. Billboard, c. 1965. Courtesy of Anheuser Busch.

136

Top: Acme Ale. Sign, 16" × 24", c. 1950. Collection of Vivian and Ira Brichta. Bottom: 7-Up. Billboard, c. 1970. The 7-Up Company.

M'm! M'm! Good! And hot!

*Campbell's Soup. Billboard, c. 1970.
Institute of Outdoor Advertising.*

ART IN THE SIXTIES

*Illustration has been identified
with American poster art since
its beginning, but during the
1960s realistic images became
a cult for many noncommercial artists too.*

*After World War II and the
decades of abstract art, artists
turned toward a "new realism"
based on the urban, gadget-
ridden society in which they
lived. To get away from art
that featured unrecognizable
shapes. Artists such as James
Rosenquist, Roy Lichtenstein,
and Andy Warhol created an
art form based on the bright
packages, comic strips, advertising billboards, and televised
commercials around them.
This artistic investigation of
the sixties' ready-made culture
was called Pop (popular) Art.*

*Andy Warhol's celebrated
paintings of Campbell Soup
cans and Alex Katz's and
James Rosenquist's flatly
painted poster people borrowed
the imagery of the skilled advertising specialists whose
work commanded the attention*

*Campbell's Soup, Andy Warhol. Oil silkscreen on canvas. 36⅛" × 24⅛", 1965. The
Museum of Modern Art.*

138

"Man and Female Nude Leaning on Chair," Philip Pearlstein. Oil on canvas, 73" square, 1970. The Art Institute of Chicago. Pearlstein's painting imitates a "cut-off" camera angle devoid of artistic editorial comment.

Top: Vincent and Tony, Alex Katz. Oil on canvas, 72" × 120", 1969. The Art Institute of Chicago. Center: Pabst's Beer. Billboard, c. 1950. Institute of Outdoor Advertising. Bottom: Swift's. Billboard, c. 1958. Institute of Outdoor Advertising. Courtesy of Swift and Company. Swift built a continuity campaign by using the same ad for many Thanksgivings. The grandfather was, for many years, the elevator operator in the building that housed McCann-Erickson, Inc., Swift's advertising agency.

of millions of people. In the past, the "fine art" painters, free to choose how they wished to paint, were willing to experiment to find new pathways in art. During the 1960s, the artists and art directors who worked in advertising studios took the lead, and their noncommercial brothers followed their initiative.

Pop artists not only depicted America's product-oriented, fast-food society, but also tested the advanced techniques of printing and photography used by commercial artists. Particularly challenging to these new converts to popular culture were the sharply defined, often brassy images found in films and advertisements and obtainable by modern color photography.

Some artists chose to imitate the work of the camera and painted peculiarly angled likenesses of people and places. Those artists built onto pop still another avenue of art, photo realism.

FOR SPEEDY THROAT RELIEF

SUCRETS

Sucrets. Poster, c. 1965. Private collection. Courtesy of Beecham Products, Division of Beecham, Inc. A poster showing the European influence of the French artist, Raymond Savignac.

NO SMOKING

Warning: The Surgeon General has determined that cigarette smoking will turn your fingers and teeth yellow, make your breath stink and ruin your lungs—do it someplace else.

Top: No Smoking. Poster, c. 1971. The anti-smoking forces continued their campaign with posters at the same time that television ads for cigarettes were banned. Bottom: Texaco. Billboard, c. 1950. Institute of Outdoor Advertising. "We Are The Men of Texaco" theme, popularized on television, found its way into outdoor posters to support the TV campaign.

TELEVISION

Advertising once meant a wide range of media: newspapers, magazines, billboards, and radio. Today, advertising to most people means television.

TV tells us what to buy and where to get it. It shows us how to keep our bathrooms fresh and our kitchens free from bugs. Television personalities set the clothing and hairstyles and furniture fashions for millions of Americans, and TV stage designers decree how our living rooms should be decorated.

At first, media gurus predicted that television would put an end to the theater and the movies and that people would not read any more. But the gurus were wrong; television, with its constant need for new material, has itself presented plays and concerts and has increased the sale of books beyond all expectations by making authors celebrities on talk shows.

Television has created celeb-

Coca-Cola. Billboard, c. 1965. Private collection. Coca-Cola is a registered trademark of the Coca-Cola Company.

Among the most successful Coca Cola programs were the posters and billboards on the theme "Things go better with Coke." Coke understood that by involving other products (hot dogs, pizza, potato chips) they would increase their own sales. The stores loved the idea, of course, since it also boosted sales of the tie-in foods. Coca-Cola didn't stop this theme with the supermarkets as they invaded fast-food and family restaurants with posters showing juicy sandwiches, chicken dinners, and platters of lobsters . . . all alleged to "go better with Coke."

rities such as Lucille Ball, Milton Berle, Ed Sullivan, Jack Paar, Johnny Carson, Carol Burnett, and Mary Tyler Moore, and has enlarged our language with words such as throw-away line, quip and confidentiality.

Although television is America's major communicator and will continue to grow as manufacturers produce increasingly sophisticated electronic equipment, magazines catering to special groups and up-to-the-moment lifestyles proliferate. Museums boast record attendances, and towns and even villages support symphony orchestras and dance troups.

Posters, while no longer the major thrust of most advertising campaigns, continue to bring the manufacturer's message to the public. And the creative, often humorous posters of today are becoming collectors' items for historians, Americana buffs and lovers of incisive illustration.

Shell Oil. Sign, c. 1950. Institute of Outdoor Advertising. New Yorker magazine cartoonist William Steig's humor was part of Shell Oil's dealer service campaign.

McDonald's. Store poster, c. 1975. McDonald's® Inc.

Libby's. Billboard, c. 1960. Institute of Outdoor Advertising.

GTE. Billboard, c. 1975. Private collection. Courtesy of GTE Service Corporation (General Telephone).

Levi's Jeans. Store poster, 1970s. Courtesy of Levi Strauss & Company.

7 Up-Company. Billboard. c. 1970.
The 7-Up Company.

Top: Sunkist. Billboard. c. 1975. Private collection. Sunkist is a trademark of Sunkist
Growers, Inc. Reprinted with permission of Sunkist Growers, Inc. Bottom: Yellow
Pages. Billboard. c. 1975. Pacific Telephone.

The Beer that Made Milwaukee Famous

om the land of sky blue waters

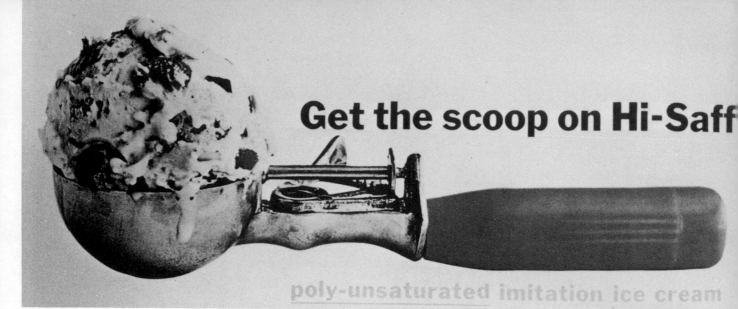

Get the scoop on Hi-Saff

poly-unsaturated imitation ice cream

High-Saff. Billboard, c. 1965. Institute of Outdoor Advertising.

Top: Sunkist. Billboard, c. 1940. Sunkist is a trade mark of Sunkist Growers, Inc. Reprinted with permission of Sunkist Growers, Inc. Bottom: Holly Sugar. Painted sign, 1960s. Foster & Kleiser. Registered trademark of Holly Sugar Corporation.

BIBLIOGRAPHY

BOOKS

Advertising: Today, Yesterday, Tomorrow. New York: McGraw-Hill Book Co., 1963.

Allen, Frederick Lewis. *The Big Change.* New York: Harper & Row, 1952.

———. *Only Yesterday: An Informal History of the 1920's.* New York: Harper & Row, 1964.

———. *Since Yesterday: The 1930's in America.* New York: Harper & Row, 1972.

Andrist, Ralph. *American Century: One Hundred Years of Changing Life Styles in America.* New York: American Heritage Press, 1972.

Annual of Advertising Art in the United States. New York: Art Directors' Club, 1921.

Barnicoat, John. *A Concise History of Posters, 1870–1970.* New York: Harry N. Abrams, 1972.

Bates, Charles Austin. *Short Talks on Advertising.* New York: Press of Charles Austin Bates, 1889.

Binder, Joseph. *Colour Advertising.* London: The Studio Ltd., 1934.

Bining, Arthur Cecil. *The Rise of American Economic Life.* New York: Charles Scribner's Sons, 1943.

Boorstin, Daniel. *The Americans: The Democratic Experience.* New York: Random House, 1973.

Byrne, Janet S. *"American Ephemera."* The Metropolitan Museum of Art *Bulletin* (April 1976).

Cahn, William. *Out of the Cracker Barrel: From Animal Crackers to ZuZu's.* New York: Simon and Schuster, 1969.

Campbell, Hannah. *Why Did They Name It?* New York: Ace Publications, 1964.

Colgate, Craig, Jr., ed. *National Trade and Professional Associations of the United States and Canada and Labor Unions.* Washington, D.C.: Columbia Books, Inc., 1979.

Crow, Carl. *The Great American Customer.* New York: Harper & Bros., 1943.

Crowley, Ellen T., ed. *Trade Names Dictionary.* Detroit: Gale Research Company, Book Tower Publishers, 1978.

DeWeese, Truman A. *Book on Advertising.* New York: The System Co., 1906.

Duce, Herbert Cecil. *Poster Advertising.* Chicago: Blakely Printing Co., 1912.

Financial Stock Guide Service. *Directory of Obsolete Securities.* New York: Financial Information, Inc., Publisher, 1978.

Fisher, Robert D. *Manuals of Extinct or Obsolete Companies.* New York: Robert D. Fisher and Marvin Scudder, Inc., Publishers, 1926 and 1937.

Flexner, James. *That Wilder Image: The Painting of America's Native School from Thomas Cole to Winslow Homer.* Boston: Little, Brown and Co., 1962.

Freeman, Larry. *Victorian Posters.* New York: American Life Foundation, 1969.

Furnas, J. C. *The Americans: A Social History of the United States, 1587–1914.* New York: G. P. Putnam's Sons, 1969.

———. *Great Times: An Informal Social History of the United States, 1914–1929.* New York: G. P. Putnam's Sons, 1974.

Gallo, Max. *The Poster in History.* New York: McGraw-Hill Book Co., 1974.

Hammond, Dorothy with Hammond, Robert. *Collectible Advertising.* Des Moines: Wallace-Homestead, 1974.

Hechtlinger, Adelaide and Cross, Wilbur. *The Complete Book of Paper Antiques.* New York: Coward, McCann and Geoghegan, 1972.

Heimann, Robert K. *Tobacco and Americans.* New York: McGraw-Hill Book Co., 1960.

Hepner, Harry Walker. *Effective Advertising.* New York: McGraw-Hill Book Co., 1941.

Hornung, Clarence P. *Handbook of Early Advertising Art.* New York: Dover Publications, 1947.

Hutchinson, Harold F. *The Poster: An Illustrated History from 1860.* New York: Viking Press, 1968.

Keady, Carolyn. *American Posters of the Turn of the Century.* New York: St. Martin's Press, 1975.

Klug, Ray. *Antique Advertising, vol. 2.* Gas City, IN: L-W Promotions, 1970.

Lewine, Harris. *Good-Bye to All That.* New York: McGraw-Hill Book Co., 1970.

Lief, Alfred. *It Floats: The Story of Procter & Gamble.* New York: Rinehart & Co., 1958.

Manufacturing Confectioners Buyer's Guide 1950–1951. Chicago: Manufacturer's Publishing Co., 1977.

Margolin, Victor. *American Poster Renaissance: The Great Age of American Poster Design, 1890–1900.* New York: Watson-Guptill, 1975.

Meadows, Cecil. *Trade Signs and Their Origin.* London: Routledge & Kegan Paul, 1957.

Mercer, F. A. and Grant, W., eds. *Modern Publicity: Commercial Art Annual.* London: The Studio Ltd., 1931.

———. *Posters and Publicity: Fine Printing and Design.* London: The Studio Ltd., 1928.

Monfred, Friedrich, and Bull, Donald, eds. *The Register of United States Breweries 1876–1976.* Stamford: Holly Press, 1976.

Parker, Paul. *"An Analysis of Style in Advertising Art"* Master's thesis, University of Chicago, 1937.

Parsons, Frank Alvah. *The Art Appeal in Display Advertising.* New York: Harper & Bros., 1921.

Powell, George H. *Powell's Practical Advertiser.* New York: George H. Powell, Publisher, 1905.

Presbrey, Frank. *The History and Development of Advertising.* New York: Doubleday, Doran & Co., 1929.

Rivers, Hugh W. *Ancient Advertising and Publicity.* Chicago: Kroch's, 1929.

Rowsome, Frank, Jr. *Think Small: The Story of Those Volkswagen Ads.* Brattleboro, VT: Stephen Greene Press, 1970.

———. *The Verse by the Side of the Road: The Story of Burma Shave Signs and Jingles.* Brattleboro, VT: Stephen Greene Press, 1965.

Sampson, Henry. *A History of Advertising from the Earliest Times.* London: Chatto and Windus, 1875.

Scott, Walter Dill. *The Psychology of Advertising.* Boston: Small, Maynard & Co., 1902.

Scull, Penrose. *From Peddlers to Merchant Princes: A History of Selling in America.* Chicago: Follett, 1967.

Street Car Advertising, Outdoor Advertising, the Advertising Agency. International Library of Technology, Scranton, PA: International Textbook Co., 1921.

Sullivan, Mark. *Our Times: The United States, 1920–1925.* 4 vols. New York: Charles Scribner's Sons, 1926–1943.

Sutphen, Dick. *The Mad Old Ads.* Minneapolis: Dick Sutphen Studio, 1966.

Toffler, Alvin. *Future Shock.* New York: Random House, 1970.

Turner, E. S. *The Shocking History of Advertising.* New York: E. P. Dutton, 1953.

Weiner, Michael A. *The Taster's Guide to Beer, Brews & Breweries of the World.* New York: Macmillan Publishing Co., Inc., 1977.

Wish, Harvey. *Contemporary America: The National Scene Since 1900.* New York: Harper & Row, 1966.

ARTICLES

Atherton, Lewis E. "The Pioneer Merchant in Mid-America." *University of Missouri Studies* vol. 14, no. 2 (1 April 1939).

Friedman, Jeannie. "WPA Poster Project: When Government Sponsors Art." *Print* July-August 1978.

"How It Was in Advertising, 1776–1976." *Advertising Age,* 19 April 1976.

"The New World of Advertising." *Advertising Age,* 21 November 1973.

The Poster. Chicago: Poster Advertising Association, 1912–1926.

Printer's Ink. 1895–1899.

Robinson, Charles Mulford. "Artistic Possibilities of Advertising." *Atlantic Monthly,* July 1904.

Signs of the Times: The National Journal of Advertising Displays, May 1956.

"Sixty Years of American Business." *Forbes,* 15 September 1977.

Acme ale, 137
Acme beer, 106
Advertising agencies, 63, 73, 122–123
Advertising Council, 133
Affluent Society, The (Galbraith), 122
Airlines, 121
Albers, Joseph, 130
All Star Kola, 108
Allen, E. C., 29
American Cereal Company, 54
American Museum, 14–15
American Navy plug tobacco, 91
American Newspaper Directory, 29
American system, 24
American Tobacco Company, 47, 72, 84
Amos 'n' Andy, 89, 106, 125
Anheuser-Busch, 25
Anti-Saloon League, 25
Apollo bicycle, 43
Armour, Phillip D., 62
Armour and Company, 62
Arrow collars and shirts, 74, 75
Art deco, 75
Assembly-line process, 8, 12
Associated Bill Posters' Association, 44
Ath-Lo-Pho-Ros, 111
Atlantic Monthly, 45, 62
Atwater Kent radio, 88
Auburn Dusenberg, 66
Aunt Jemima pancake flour, 34, 125
Automobiles, 27, 43–44, 56, 65–66, 119–121, 123, 127–129, 132, 134
Averill Chemical Paint Company, 32
Ayer, N. W., and Son, 31

Babbitt, B. J., Best soap, 52
Bachman, Charlie, 38, 39, 42
Bailey, F., 6
Baker electric vehicles, 66
Baker horse blanket, 51
Ball Costumes cigarettes, 48
Barbed wire, 26
Barn painting, 35, 36
Barnum, P. T., 14–15, 29, 37, 76
Barton, Bruce, 73
Bass, Saul, 130
Bathroom fixtures, 55
Bathtubs, 17, 55
Battle Ax Plug, 35
Bayer, Herbert, 130
Beatles, 124
Beech-nut fruit drops, 110
Beech-nut gum, 110
Beeman's pepsin-flavored gum, 131
Beer, 25, 86, 91
Beggarstaffs, 41
Bell, Alexander Graham, 26
Bell Telephone, 81
Bella Mundo cigars, 83
Benz, Carl, 43–44

Bergdoll, Louis, Brewing Company, 25
Berkeley, William, 4
Bernbach, Dave, 129
Bernhard, Lucien, 75
Bernhardt, Andreas, 136
Bicycle manufacturers, 43
Big Mac, 122, 136
Big Spring whiskey, 53
Billboards, 44–45, 74–76
Billposting, 37
Billsticking, 37
Bismarck table beer, 99
Bitters, 25
Black Jack gum, 131
Blacks, 33, 125–126
Bock beer, 91
Boeing's 707 jet, 121
Bon-Tons cigarettes, 85
Borden, Gail, 57
Borden's ice cream, 57
Borden's milk, 57
Boston *News-Letter*, 4
Bow, Clara, 68, 69
Bradbury and Houghteling, 35, 36
Bradley, Will, 42, 43
Brand image, 129
Breweries, 25
Bromo-Seltzer, 67, 109
Bruant, Aristide, 42
Bubbles (Millais), 41
Buckland, Doctor, Scotch Oats Essence, 49
Budweiser, 136
Buffalo Rock ginger ale, 102
Buick, 66
Bull Durham tobacco, 35, 47
Bunner, H. C., 40
Burma Shave, 82–83
Burpee seeds, 31
Butterick, E., and Company, 22

Cadillac, 66
Camels cigarettes, 71, 72, 59–60
Campbell's soup, 85, 138
Campfire marshmallows, 65
Canadian Illustrated News, 42
Canned food, 24
Canning, 20
Carbonated water, 24
Carleton and Kissam, 38
Carlu, Jean, 75
Carnation milk, 35
Carter, Boake, 89
Carter's Little Liver pills, 30
Cash register, 27
Cassandre, A. M., 75
Castle, Irene, 85
Cat's Paw rubber heels, 67
Caxton, William, 4
Centennial Exhibition (Philadelphia, 1876), 26, 43
Centlivre tonic, 103
Cereals, 24, 54
Chain stores, 27, 64, 120
Chambers, Charles E., 75
Champion American soap powder, 13
Checker taxi, 112
Chéret, Jules, 41

Cherry Smash, 91
Chesterfield cigarettes, 71, 72, 75, 78, 98
Chevrolet, 65–66, 134
Chewing gum, 131
Chromolithography, 39–41
Chromos, 39
Chrysler, 66, 120, 121
Cigarettes, 46–47, 71–72, 84–85, 130
Cigars, 46, 47
Circus posters, 15
Civil War, 21, 24, 35
Civilian Conservation Corps, 78
Cloth of Gold cigarettes, 85
Clothing industry, 19, 21–23
Cloverbloom butter, 105
Cluett and Peabody's Arrow shirts and collars, 74, 75
Coca-Cola, 24, 25, 58, 59, 61, 141
Cocoa, 19
Coffee, 14
Colgate Company, 53
Colin, Paul, 75
Colonel Sanders, 122
Columbia bicycle, 31, 43
Conestoga wagons, 12
Conspicuous consumption, 119
Consumer movement, 132
Consumer Reports, 80
Consumer's Research, Inc., 79
Consumer's Union, 80
Continental Baking Company, 132–133
Coolidge, Calvin, 66
Cooper, Fred, 76
Corliss, Henry, 26
Correctol, 130
Corvair, 132
Cosmetics industry, 69
Cough drops, 32
Council of National Defense, 67
Country stores, 13–14
Cox, Palmer, 62
Crapper, Thomas, 55
Cream of Wheat, 90
Credit cards, 124
Creel, George, 67
Creel Committee, 67
Creigh, John, 6
Creole cigarettes, 47
Crowell, Henry, 54
Crystal Palace Exhibition, 26
Currier, Nathaniel, 39
Currier and Ives, 39–40
Curtis, Cyrus K., 128
Cusak, Thomas, 35
Cutty Sark, 76
Cycle cigarettes, 46
Cycling, 43

Daily News, 128
Daimler, Gottlieb, 43
Darling (car), 66
Davis, Perry, Vegetable Pain Killer, 33
Day, Stephen, 4
De Mille, Cecil B., 71
Deane's evening clothes for men, 102
Dearlove, Fidelia, 82–83

Depression, 77–79
Diehl, Christian, Brewing Company, 101
Dionne quintuplets, 74, 108
Divan Japonais, 42
Division of Advertising of Committee of Public Information, 67
Dobbelmann, Louis, Tabak, 47
Dodge, 66, 119
Doublemint gum, 131
Doublemint twins, 131
Drive-in market, 65
Duck Foot tires, 99
Duke, Buck, 84
Duke, Washington, 47
Duke Tobacco Company, 45, 47
Duryea, Charles, 43
Duryea's corn starch, 35

Eagle Brand, 57
Eastman, George, 59–60
Eastman Company, 59
Ebony, 126
Edison, Thomas, 27
Eighteenth Amendment, 70
Electric furnace, 27
Electric signs, 76–77
Elsie the Cow, 57
England, 41, 42
Erie Canal, 12
Erla radio, 88
Essex, 66
Estrella cigarettes, 85

Factories, early, 12
Fairbank, N. B., Company, 33, 54
Fairy soap, 31, 94
Falstaff, 86
Fast-food franchisers, 121–122
Federal Deposit Insurance Corporation, 78
Federal Trade Commission, 74, 80, 132, 133
Felco pearls, 102
Ferry seeds, 31, 35
Fillmore, Millard, 55
Fisk tires, 66, 74, 76, 104
Fixed-price policy, origin of, 15
Flagg, James Montgomery, 90
Floethe, Richard, 78
Flour, 19
Flyer cigar, 96
Food Administration, 67
Food and Drug Act, 14, 64
Food industry, 19, 20
Ford, 111, 120, 121, 124, 135
Ford, Henry, 8, 44, 65, 66
Foster, John, 6
Fowler, Nathaniel, 31
Franken, Richard B., 20
Franklin (car), 66
Franklin, Benjamin, 4–5
Free-trial, 11
Friends oats, 57
Furness, Betty, 132

Galaxy, The, 30
Galbraith, John Kenneth, 122
Garland, 66
General Foods, 123
General Motors, 65, 66, 120, 121, 124, 129, 132, 134
General store, 13–14
General Telephone, 143
Glaser, Milton, 132

Gold Dust cleanser, 31, 33
Gold Dust Twins, 33
Golden Age cigarettes, 85
Golden Rule stores, 27
Goodrich, B. F., 81
Goodyear, 66
Great Atlantic and Pacific Tea Company (A & P), 27, 64
Great Atlantic Tea Company, 27
Green Giant peas, 81
Griffin, Burr, 76
Grove's Tasteless Chill tonic, 51
Gude, O. J., 35, 77
100,000,000 Guinea Pigs, 79
Gund's Peerless beverage, 86
Gunning, R. J., 35
Gutenberg, Johannes, 4

Halftone printing, 42–43
Hall, Dr. P., catarrh remedy, 49
Hall's hair renewer, 49
Hamm's beer, 145
Harper's, 42
Harte, Bret, 30
Hartford, George Huntington, 27
Haskell's wheat flakes, 24
Haynes (car), 66
Health Jolting chair, 49
Heinz, H. J., 24
Heinz, H. J., Company, 76
Heinz baked beans, 65
Henry J (car), 120
Highway Beautification Act, 127
Highwheeler, 43
Hill, George Washington, 72, 84–85
Hires, Charles G., 24
Hi-Saff, 146
Hoardings, 37
Hoffman, Jacob, Brewing Company, 103
Hohlwein, Ludwig, 75
Holiday Inn, 122
Holly sugar, 146
Hommel, M., champagne, 101
Honest copy, 29
Hoods' sarsaparilla, 35, 42
Hoover, Herbert, 67, 77
Hopkins, Claude, 129
Hornby's oatmeal, 24
Horton's, washing machines, 100
Hostetter, Dr., bitters, 50
Houghteling, "Hote," 35
Howe, Elias, 21
Hudson, 121

Incandescent lamp, 27
Indians, tobacco shop, 1, 8, 45–46
Industrial Revolution, 26
Installment buying, 12, 124
Interchangeable parts, 24
International Advertising Association, 66
International Society for Christian Endeavor, 72
Ipana, 89
Irwin, Wallace, 69
Ives, Frederick E., 42–43
Ives, J. Merritt, 39
Ivory soap, 35, 40, 41, 52–53, 72

Jack in the Box, 136
Jantzen swimming suits, 87

Jelke Good Luck margarine, 115
Jell-O, 89
Jenner, Bruce, 74
Jet, 126
Jewett, 66
Joan of Arc kidney beans, 56
Johnson, Caleb, 53
Johnson, Howard, restaurants, 121–122
Johnson, Lyndon, 125
Jones, John Beauchamp, 13
Jordan (car), 66

Kaiser, Henry J., 120
Kaiser Aluminum Company, 120
Kaltenborn, H. V., 89
Katz, Alex, 138
Kawasaki, 129
Kellet, Arthur, 79
Kellogg, 123
Kennedy Medical Discovery poster, 49
Kirschbaum clothes, 84
Kissam and Allen, 37
Kissel (car), 66
Kitchen fixtures, 55
Knowlton, E. J., 17
Knowlton's bathing apparatus, 17
Kodak, 30, 59–60, 67
Korbel Sec champagne, 106
Korean War, 121
Kraft Foods, 62
Kroc, Ray, 122
Kuppenheimer Good Clothes, 73

La Corona cigars, 47
La Diaphane powder, 41
Ladies Home Journal, 128
Lager beer, 25
Lambert, Warner, 132
Larabee, Carroll B., 20
Lasker, Albert, 30, 72, 84
Lava soap, 89
League of American Wheelmen, 43
Leased hoardings, 37
Level Head tobacco, 48
Lever Brothers, 73
Levi's, 131, 143
Levy's rye bread, 131
Leyendecker, J. C., 42, 66, 74, 75
Libby's pineapple, 143
Libby's specialties, 65
Lichtenstein, Roy, 138
Life, 127
Life and Letters of Sir John Millais (Millais), 41
Lifebuoy soap, 73
Life-Savers, 111
Lincoln (car), 66
Lindbergh, Charles, 74
Lippincott's, 42
Listerine, 132
Literary men, 29
Lithography, 38–42
Loewy, Raymond, 120
London *Times*, 17
Look, 127
Lord, D. M., 62
Lord and Taylor, 38
Lord and Thomas advertising agency, 30
Lorillard, Pierre, 45
Lorillard's snuff, 48
Luck of Roaring Camp, The (Harte), 30
Lucky Strike cigarettes, 50, 72, 84–85

McCormick reaper, 17–19, 41
McDonald's, 122, 136, 142
McKay machine, 23
Macbeth lamp chimneys, 30
Macy, R. H., 15
Macy's department store, 15, 17, 27
Magazines, 127–128
Mail Pouch tobacco, 35, 93
Man Nobody Knows, The (Barton), 73
Manhattan Project, 80
Manoli cigarettes, 75
Mapes, Emery, 90
Marathon lager beer, 82
Market Facts, Inc., 123
Market research, 64
Marlboro cigarettes, 129
Marlboro shirts and sportswear, 123
Marmon (car), 66
Marschall, A., and Company, 54
Marshall Field and Company, 27, 120
Marvels cigarettes, 97
Mass production, 21, 67
Mastodon Air-tight cooking range, 16, 17
Mathew, Richard, 6
Mattel, 123
Matter, Herbert, 130
Maxwell, 66
Medical quackery, 49–50
Mentholatum, 108
Merrill Lynch, 130
Merrimack Manufacturing Company, 21
Metropolitan Opera Company, 72
Mill, The (Otis), 39
Millais, John, 41
Miller Brewing Company, 86
Minimalist art, 130–131
Mobilgas, 107
Model A, 66
Model T, 65, 66, 134
Moholy-Nagy, Lazlo, 130
Morgan, Matt, 40
Morris, Philip, 47, 72, 82
Morris, William, 42
Morse, Samuel, 5
Morton salt, 34–35, 137
Moscoso, Victor, 131
Motel business, 121, 122
Motion pictures, 71, 124
Moxie, 104
Mozart cigar, 96
Murad and Helmer cigarettes, 72
Murphy varnishes, 30, 52
Myerson, Bess, 132

Nader, Ralph, 132
Nader's Raiders, 132
Nash, 121
National Biscuit Company, 88, 89, 110, 116
Neuman's ice cream, 104
Neville, George Washington, 69
New Deal, 78
New York Advertising Sign Company, 36
New York *Graphic*, 42
New York *Herald*, 5
New York *World*, 76
Niagara Falls, 36
Nicholson, William, 42
Nielson, A. C., and Company, 123
Nineteenth Amendment, 69
Ny-Quil, 130

Odell, Leonard and Allan, 82–83
Office of War Information, 81
Official Five Cent cigar, 35
Old Dutch cleanser, 33
Olds, R. E., 44
Opera Puffs cigarettes, 85
Otis, Bass, 39
Outdoor advertising, 35, 36, 44–45, 75, 76
Ovaltine, 89
Overland, 66, 82
Overman Wheel Company, 43
Owen, 66

Pabst beer, 139
Pabst Brewing Company, 81
Packages That Sell (Franken and Larabee), 20
Packaging, 19–20, 64, 136
Packard (car), 66, 121
Packer's tar soap, 98
Packing, 20
Paintings, 41
Pal Ade, 109
Palmer, Volney, 29
Palmolive soap, 53, 73, 75, 92, 126
Palmolive Soap Company, 53
Paris garters and suspenders, 112
Parker fountain pen, 74
Parlin, Charles Coolidge, 63–64
Parmelee System cabs, 112
Parrish, Maxfield, 42, 43, 74
Patent medicines, 14, 29, 31, 35, 36, 49, 62, 64
Pattison, Edward and William, 9
Pears Company, 53
Pears soap, 41, 53, 94
Peddlers, 9, 11, 12
Peerless washboards, 51
Penfield, Edward, 42, 66
Pennsylvania Gazette, The, 5
Pepsodent toothpaste, 84, 106
Pettijohn's California breakfast food, 55
Philadelphia, 1, 2, 3, 17, 26
Philco radio, 88
Phonograph, 27
   records, 71
Photo realism, 139
Photography, 59–60, 76, 128
Photo-offset printing process, 76
Pierce-Arrow (car), 66
Piggly Wiggly, 64
Pinkham, Lydia E., 49–50
   vegetable compound, 49–50
Pioneer baskets, 107
Plug chewing tobacco, 45
Plumbing, 55
Plymouth, 135
Pontiac, 66
   Grand Prix, 134
Pop art, 138–139
Pope, Albert, 43
Pope Manufacturing Company, 43
Posters, 7, 14–15, 19–20, 37–43, 75, 130, 141
Powell, George, 49
Powers, John, 29–30, 44
Practical Advertiser (Powell), 49

Prang and Company, 40
Pratt, Matthew, 3
Preservation of food, 20
Presley, Elvis, 123, 124
Preston and Merrill, 19, 20
Priester matches, 75
Priestley, Joseph, 24
Process engraving, 42
Procter, Harley, 40, 52
Procter & Gamble, 31, 41, 52–53, 121
Prohibition, 69, 70, 86
Pryde, James, 42
Psyche, 126
Psychology of Advertising, The (Scott), 62
Publicity, 62
Puritan tailors, 95

Quackery, 49–50
Quaker oats, 24, 34, 54, 74, 108
Quaker Oats Company, 54
Quaker Wheat Berries, 54
Quarter Pounder, 142
Quiz shows, 123

Radio, 71, 88–89, 124
Railroads, 27, 38
Raleigh, Walter, 1
Raleigh cigarettes, 62, 97
Rand, Paul, 130
Rastus, 90, 125
RCA radio, 88
Ready-made clothing, 19, 21–23
Red Dot cigars, 97
Red Man tobacco, 114
Reed, Ethel, 42
Refrigerators, 17, 65, 127
Regensburg's Havana cigars, 96
Remington Agricultural Works, 10
Remington typewriters, 86
Reo, 66, 91
Revlon, 123, 126
Revson, Charles, 126
Reynolds, R. J., 72
Rhead, Louis, 42
Rice Electrical Display Company, 77
Robinson, Charles Milford, 45
Rock painting, 35, 36
Rockwell, Norman, 75–76
Rocky Mountain News, 67
Roi-Tan cigars, 47
Rolfe, John, 45
Roosevelt, Franklin Delano, 78
Root beer syrup, 24
Rosenheim's bitters, 25
Rosenquist, James, 138
Rowell, George P., 29
Rowntree's Elect cocoa, 42
Royal baking powder, 30, 101, 113
Royal Crown Cola, 79
Royal Tailors, 85

Safety bicycle, 43
St. Jacob's oil, 35, 36, 37
Sala, George, 38
Sandwich boards, 37
Sapolio laundry soap, 30, 31, 38
Sarony, Knapp and Major, 40
Satin skin cream and powder, 95
Saturday Evening Post, 58, 63, 76, 113, 127
Saxoleine lamps, 41
Schlink, F. J., 79
Schlitz, Joseph, 25

Schlitz beer, 145
Scott, Walter Dill, 62–63
Scribner's, 42
Sears, Richard Warren, 29
Sears, Roebuck and Company, 29, 120, 121
Self-service food stores, 64
Senfelder, Alois, 38
Serial advertising, 62
Seven-Up, 131, 132, 137, 144
Sewage systems, 55
Sewing machine, 21
Sheik, The, 71
Shell Motor Oil, 110, 142
Shepard, Otis, 130, 131
Shepard Chapin and Company, 17
Shoe machinery, 23–24
Shoes, 23
Shopping centers, 120
Shoudy, G. A. and Son, soap, 50
Sign painters, 35
Singer sewing machines, 30, 31
Siquis (Caxton), 4
Sitting Bull smoking tobacco, 46
Slater, Samuel, 12
Sloan, Alfred, 65–66, 129
Sloan, John, 43
Slogans, 34–35
Smith Brothers cough drops, 32
Smokey the Bear, 133
Soap manufacturers, 52–53, 72–73
Soda pop, 24
Soft drinks, 25, 58
Spirit of St. Louis, 74
Spring and Company, 56
S T 1860, 36
Standard Oil Company, 60
Star soap, 53, 94
Statler Hotel (Buffalo, N.Y.), 55
Steam engine, 26
Steam turbine, 27
Steamboat, 12
Steinway, 30
Stern Knight, 66
Stewart, A. T., 13, 15, 17, 19
Stewart's department store, 13, 15, 17
Stewart-Warner radios, 70, 88
Stiller shoes, 75
Stimpson, Edwin B., shoe machinery, 23
Stopette spray deodorant, 123
Straights, 23
Strauss, Levi, and Company, 34, 131, 132
Strawbridge and Clothier, 100
Streetcar advertising, 38
Strobridge Lithographic Company, 40–41
Studebaker, 120
Sucrets, 140

Suffolk Brewing Company, 103
Sugar, 19
Sunkist, 144
Sunoco, 105
Supermarket, 65
Sweet, Orr and Company's Pantaloon Overalls, 34
Sweet Caporal cigarettes, 85
Swift's Premium, 90, 117, 128, 139

Tabak, 47
Tanlac, 116
Target tobacco, 98
Tea, 14, 19
Telephone, 26, 123
Television, 117, 123, 124, 130, 140–141
Templar (car), 66
Terry, Eli, 11–12, 124
Terry clock, 11–12
Testimonial advertising, 73–74
Texaco, 140
Texas Pacific Coal and Oil Company, 114
Theory of the Leisure Class, The (Veblen), 26
Thomas, Lowell, 89
Thompson, J. Walter, 29, 31
Ti-con-der-oga school supplies, 104
Tin Lizzies, 65
Tires, 66
Tobacco, 35, 45–47, 130
Tobacco shop figures, 1, 8, 45–46
Toffler, Alvin, 133
Toiletine, 116
Toulouse-Lautrec, Henri, 41, 42
Trademarks, 32–35
Treidler, Adolph, 76
Trolley car, 27
Truth in Packaging, 136
Tryon, E. K., Jr., Company, 43
Tugwell, Rexford, 80
Tuttle's Horse Elixir, 107
Tutts pills, 35
Twenty-first Amendment, 70

Uncle Tom's Cabin (Stowe), 40–41
Underwood, Clarence G., 75
Uneeda Biscuits, 88, 89
United Airlines, 121
United States Patent Office, 26, 32
Universal Percolator, 89
Unsafe at Any Speed (Nader), 132

Valentino, Rudolph, 71
Vanity Fair cigarettes, 85
Veblen, Thorstein, 26
Victor collar button, 113

Victor and Victoria cycles, 42, 43, 56
Vietnam War, 125
Virginia Leaf tobacco, 46
Virginia Slims cigarettes, 129–130
Volkswagen, 129, 131, 135
Volstead Act, 70

Walker, Asa, 11
Wanamaker, John, 21–22, 30, 31
Wanamaker's department store, 27, 30
War Advertising Council, 81
Ward, Aaron Montgomery, 27–28, 31
Ward, Montgomery, and Company, 27–28
Warhol, Andy, 138
Washington, George, 46
Water White Electric Oil, 60
W. B. Corsets, 113
Welch's drink, 105
Wesley, John, 2
West, Benjamin, 3
Western Merchant, The (Jones), 13
Westward the Course of Empire, 41
Wheaties, 74, 89
Wheatlet, 20
Wheeler-Lee Amendment, 80
Whiskey, 25, 86
White, Charles III, 132
White House coffee, 98
White Rock sparkling beverages, 126
Whitehead, Walter, 90
Whiting's Standard papers, 42
Whitney, Eli, 8, 24
Wilcox, Jessie, 90
Wild West Show, 15
Willardson, Dave, 132
Willys (car), 66
Wilson, Kemmons, 122
Wilson, Woodrow, 67, 68
Wine, 25, 86
Winston, 66
Winston cigarettes, 62
Wizard oil, 35
Wolcott, Alexander, 83
Wolfe, Bruce, 131
Women, 23, 68–70, 72, 85, 126–127
Wonder bread, 132
Woodbury soap, 73
Woodcuts, 6, 14, 15, 42
Woolworth, Frank, 27
Works Project Administration, 78
Poster Project, 78
World War II, 78–79, 80
Wrigley, William, 130
Wrigley's gum, 77, 130
Wyeth, N. C., 90

Yellow Pages, 144

Zaid, Barry, 132